Trends in Charitable Giving
for the 21st Century

Edited by
Catherine Walker and Cathy Pharoah
with Pauline Jas, Andrew Passey and Debbie Romney-Alexander

Hodder & Stoughton

A MEMBER OF THE HODDER HEADLINE GROUP

Editor Andrew Steeds

Typesetting Fakenham Photosetting Ltd

A catalogue record for this book is available from the British Library

ISBN 0–340–80491–2

The CAF research team
Cathy Pharoah
Catherine Walker
Debbie Romney-Alexander
Michelle Graley
Web address http://www.CAFonline.org/research

Charities Aid Foundation
Kings Hill
West Malling
Kent
ME19 4TA
Tel +44 (0) 1732 520000
Fax +44 (0) 1732 520001
Web address http://www.CAFonline.org

Printed in Great Britain for Hodder & Stoughton Educational, a division of Hodder Headline plc, 338 Euston Road, London NW1 3BH by The Bath Press Ltd, Bath.

CONTENTS

Foreword *Michael Brophy*   v

List of abbreviations   vi

1 Charities and individual giving today
  Cathy Pharoah   1

2 The evolution of charitable giving *Redmond Mullin*   8

3 How much do people give to charity, and who are the
  donors? *Cathy Pharoah*   23

4 Fundraising methods – how people give   43
  How the general public gives *Pauline Jas*   43
  Boxed in? Strategies for fundraising from individuals
  Joe Saxton   49
  The potential of the internet for future charitable giving
  Howard Lake   56
  Where now for legacy fundraising? *Richard Radcliffe*   60

5 The tax return – giving tax-effectively   65
  An overview of tax-effective giving *Cathy Pharoah and*
  Catherine Walker   66
  Payroll giving: access to charitable tax reliefs through the
  payroll *Debbie Romney-Alexander*   83
  Taxing times in a brave new world? Opportunities and
  difficulties posed by the millennium tax changes
  Mark Robson   90

6 Worthy causes? What do donors give to?   102
  What makes a cause worth giving to? *Les Hems*   102
  From marketing products to fundraising for causes
  Stephen Lee   109
  The importance of the public's trust and confidence in
  charities *Andrew Passey*   115
  Relating to new donors *Stephen Pidgeon*   120
  Donor profiling *Cathy Pharoah*   127

7 Altruism, guilt and the feel-good factor – why do people give
  to charity? *Catherine Walker*   134

8 What turns donors on? What turns them off? *Adrian Sargeant* 162

9 What future for giving?   180
   The credibility of charity *Richard Fries*   180
   A memorandum on the globalisation of future
   philanthropy *David Wickert*   183
   The donor–charity deal *John Kingston*   185
   The electronic future *Sarah Hughes*   189
   The future of civil society *Barry Knight*   191

10 End-note: redefining charity *Cathy Pharoah, Catherine
    Walker, Pauline Jas and Andrew Passey*   197

About the authors   203

Useful addresses   211

About CAF   214

About NCVO   215

FOREWORD
Michael Brophy

I am very proud of CAF's role in developing *A Lot of Give*. In fact, it gives me the kind of 'warm glow' described in Catherine Walker's particularly interesting chapter on why people give. 'People feel good when they give to charity, and the more they give the better they feel.' Down-to-earth stuff, but it sounds right.

It may seem rather a cliché to write that this book is essential reading for anyone concerned with or about levels of giving in the UK. Nonetheless I write it, because I think in this case it rings true. Not only is this book of great practical use to those interested in maintaining and raising present levels of giving, but it is also of use to those with an academic interest in the subject – and to others with a more general interest, because it brings together so much within its covers.

So, it answers questions about why people give, how much they give and how they might be persuaded to give more. But more than that – and of great interest to me – it gets into the new seam of support for charities, namely *social investment*. The case for social investment is based on a number of premises, not least that, as people become more knowledgeable about social needs and closer to the ways in which charitable activity can bring about change, they will wish to have a relationship more akin to that of investment than philanthropy. People are able to invest more than they can give. And keep final control of their money.

I am particularly pleased to see the role of foundations discussed and the need for them to play the same kind of role in the UK that they play in the US. They are well placed to take the strategic view and to provide funding to implement changes in attitude and practice. What is missing in Britain is a Ford Foundation; some of us had hoped this might be the Community Fund, but government increasingly has taken a different view of its role. If foundations lead, charities and public giving and investment will follow. But it doesn't happen. Not yet anyway.

This book is timely, therefore. Philanthropy retains a small foothold in this country: individual giving represents well under one per cent of individual income. Frequent comparisons are made between the percentage of income given by people in this country and that given by people in the US. I am not sure whether this direct comparison is meaningful, but certainly to raise levels of giving closer to 1 per cent of people's income, as the Giving Campaign is trying to do, does not seem to me too high an aspiration, given the range of new tax incentives and the increasing sophistication of charities in 'making the ask'.

Barry Knight's last paragraph in the penultimate chapter tells it all: funding policies should 'put an end to the present sense of muddling along and vaguely doing good. What was good enough in the charitable sector in the twentieth century will not meet the demands of the twenty-first century.'

In that sense, this book adds a clarion call for action to the other attributes I've alluded to.

Michael Brophy
Chief Executive, CAF
December 2001

LIST OF ABBREVIATIONS

ACF	Association of Charitable Foundations
BSA	British Social Attitudes
CAF	Charities Aid Foundation
CCI	Corporate Community Investment
CEMVO	Council of Ethnic Minority Voluntary Sector Organisations
CGT	Capital Gains Tax
CSR	Corporate Social Responsibility
CTR	Charities Tax Review
DRTV	Direct Response Television
EMF	Ethnic Minority Foundation
FES	Family Expenditure Survey
GAYE	Give As You Earn
GDP	Gross Domestic Product
ICFM	Institute of Charity Fundraising Managers
IFS	Institute of Fiscal Studies
IGS	Individual Giving Survey
IR	Inland Revenue
ISP	Internet Service Provider
JPR	Institute for Jewish Policy Research
JRF	Joseph Rowntree Foundation
NCVO	National Council for Voluntary Organisations
NOP	National Opinion Poll
PAYE	Pay As You Earn
PFO	Professional Fundraising Organisation
PIU	Performance and Innovation Unit

1 CHARITIES AND INDIVIDUAL GIVING TODAY

Cathy Pharoah

Charitable giving is one of our oldest impulses and fundraising one of our oldest professions, as Redmond Mullin shows in an opening chapter of this book. An act that may be at once instinctual, moral, social, institutional and economic, the making of a charitable gift has received scattered attention in many literatures and comprehensive consideration in none. The material presented in this book attempts to pull together in one place a wide range of current information, data and thinking about charitable giving. It is intended as a resource book for all those interested or involved in promoting giving.

Such a resource is timely. The charity world in Britain is feeling the winds of change as its borders with private and public sectors open. Companies are under pressure to adopt the traditional charity values of social inclusion and responsibility. Charities are under pressure to emulate the efficiency and commercial success of companies. Meanwhile, government is exploring the potential of the non-profit sector as a partner in the delivery of core social and economic welfare programmes. What is the role of public individual giving to charities within these shifting boundaries? How does the public perceive the role of charities today? More importantly, do shifting perceptions influence the public's willingness to support charities?

The main focus of this book is on trends in charitable gift giving by individuals in Britain today, and not on gifts made by companies or private foundations, which need separate studies of their own (reference to these is made, however, where they cross over with individual giving). Gifts from individuals are the face of charitable funding most familiar to the British public, and make up a large proportion of many major charities' funding.

With the proportion of the public who give to charities declining, the need to understand giving better has become urgent. The question of why people should give to charity today needs fresh answers. As government seeks a new definition of charity to encompass the voluntary sector's roles in economic regeneration and service delivery, voluntary organisations seek a new meaning for charity relevant to a more secular, consumerist and democratic public. There is little comfort with Victorian charitable dependence.

How is a new culture of giving to be created? A number of strong currents are moving through the British voluntary sector that will influence future relationships with donors. New fiscal measures to stimulate giving have been introduced by a government committed to reviving a sense of individual responsibility towards the community. This is part of a global awareness of the importance of a healthy civil society, where voluntary and community organisations play a large role. Government and the voluntary sector are working together in a practical way through a joint Giving Campaign to promote giving.[1] Traditional notions of charities are giving way to new concepts such as 'social enterprise'; traditional 'gifts' are giving way to notions of 'venture philanthropy' and 'social investment'. These ideas have been born out of growing social concern for sustainable change, and the possible role of charities, and voluntary and community organisations, in bringing this about. Public perceptions of charities are being addressed through a new awareness among charity managers of the need for transparency and accountability in what they do, and to strengthen public trust and confidence in charities. The new media are bringing an increasingly well-informed public access to first-hand knowledge of local, national and international charitable organisations. Potential donors are faced with needs on a global scale and with many new opportunities for giving. The converse to this is that charities have new global opportunities for fundraising.[2] Britain is estimated to have the fourth-largest non-profit sector in the world in terms of revenue and is an important leader in international giving.

---

[1] *The Giving Campaign, launched in July 2001, is an independent national campaign supported by the voluntary sector and the government. It has been established to increase the amount of money given to UK charities mainly through increasing awareness and promotion of tax-effective giving.*

[2] *One new group to have seized the opportunities presented by the internet, for example, is the activists who have found a new and effective way of organising themselves for intervention on global causes.*

Such trends are forging a different discourse for philanthropy. Many of the contributors to this book are shaping fresh visions, and a new contract with donors. In moving forward, however, it is vital to start with a sense of where we are now, and what the current trends are. The framework of the book, therefore, is a set of basic questions:

- How much do individuals give to charity today?
- Who gives to charity today?
- What are the main ways in which the public gives to charity?
- Which causes does the public support?
- Why do people give to charity?
- How will the future of charitable giving look?

The aim of the book is to provide up-to-date information in each of these areas, with commentary on the main trends. To achieve this, certain contributors were asked to provide a summary of current data and research on individual giving under each of those topic areas, while others were asked to contribute commentaries and opinion pieces largely from their personal and professional experience of either raising gifts directly or providing strategic fundraising and marketing advice. The material in the book therefore consists of different types of contribution. Where Catherine Walker, Cathy Pharoah, Andrew Passey, Pauline Jas, Les Hems, Debbie Romney-Alexander and Adrian Sargeant have focused principally on the empirical research, Joe Saxton, Richard Radcliffe, Stephen Lee and Stephen Pidgeon have provided opinion pieces on the main trends. Redmond Mullin, Howard Lake and Mark Robson have provided overviews of particular areas with some commentary. The authors in Chapter 9 were asked specifically to contribute their own visions of issues crucial for the future of individual giving to charity.

Although the content is structured along the main topics of who gives what to charity, and how and why gifts are made, inevitably certain themes cut across several areas. Donations and fundraising, for example, are two sides of the same coin: it is virtually impossible to dissociate donations from the way in which they are made, with the result that fundraising techniques (including public relations, communications and marketing) are addressed throughout the book. No apology is made for this, since the central focus of the book is individual gifts of money to charities. Some topics are dealt with in greater detail than others simply because the availability of research and data is extremely variable.

It is not possible to address broader theoretical questions satisfactorily in a project aimed principally at providing an overview of current applied research. With its pragmatic focus on the state of giving today, this book contains, for example, little critique of common assumptions. Only passing references are made to the different insights brought to giving by the various disciplines within which it has been studied, and how these might – or might not – fit together. The very large anthropological literature on giving is likely to be a particularly rich source for insights into charitable giving. Perspectives on issues such as what 'charity' and 'charities' mean within different cultural and historical contexts, and how such meanings affect giving, could add enormously to our understanding of giving. They remain exciting tasks for future research on a topic that we hope will receive increasing attention.

Within the British context, the terms 'charity', 'voluntary sector', 'community sector', and 'non-profit sector' are all used in discussion and research, depending on the varying emphases required. No attempt has been made within this book to impose a single terminology or set of definitions on this fluid use of terms. This is not because it is regarded as simply a semantic issue. The main reason is a pragmatic one. It is often convenient to refer to 'the voluntary sector', although many organisations that might be included under this heading are not fundraising charities. 'The voluntary sector' is not a single entity but a set of overlapping sectors in which it is sometimes more helpful to concentrate on common characteristics, and sometimes on differences. This book does not claim to be about the voluntary sector as a whole, but only about that part of it concerned with individual donating.

About this book

The book opens with Redmond Mullin's historical review of charitable giving (Chapter 2), showing long traditions in, for example, the role of philanthropy in major public and civic projects, the part played by fundraisers and the variable relationship between what people give and what they can afford. Redmond Mullin argues there is huge scope for greater giving today, and that there is plenty of historical precedent for generosity. Following this brief scene setting, the next set of chapters focuses on aspects of giving money today. In Chapter 3, Cathy Pharoah makes a new assessment of the evidence available from different sources on amounts given and concludes that a consistent picture is emerging in which a decreasing proportion of givers are giving ever-larger gifts. This may pose a dilemma for charities, which have to choose between an undesirable decline in democratic support and a desirable shrinking of fundraising costs.

In Chapter 4, Pauline Jas provides a comparison of the success of various fundraising mechanisms today in raising money and their variable return on investment. She argues, however, that different mechanisms appeal to different types of donor and that this needs to be taken into account in any cost–benefit analysis. The use of new media for new methods of marketing and fundraising is covered in detail by Joe Saxton, and Howard Lake provides a thorough map of internet fundraising and donor development. Richard Radcliffe takes a specific look at legacy fundraising, tackling head-on the rather ambiguous attitudes of fundraisers towards an area that has been hugely successful for charities but is often not incorporated into mainstream fundraising strategy.

The discussion of mechanisms for giving is completed with a detailed review of tax-effective giving in Chapter 5 by Cathy Pharoah, Catherine Walker, Debbie Romney-Alexander and Mark Robson. Tax-effective giving techniques are shown to have the greatest scope for raising large gifts, and opportunities for their use have been extended significantly in recent government fiscal measures. Their success, however, is hampered by limited public use and understanding of the tax benefits. Mark Robson reviews the overall impact of various tax reliefs on the sector. Ways of promoting tax-effective giving are suggested, based on detailed research of its impact.

Pauline Jas notes (in her contribution to Chapter 4) that different causes are supported through different ways of giving. Chapter 6 moves on to the question of what causes the public supports. Les Hems looks at the evidence on what the public supports and provides some fresh insights into what types of marketing have been most successful for different causes, drawing on cross-cultural comparisons with the USA. It is arguable that public attitudes towards charities are as significant for giving as actual mechanisms. Andrew Passey draws attention to a loss of public trust and confidence in the sector, which may be inhibiting a growth in support. He argues that there is a tension between the public's faith in what charities do and their distrust of the way some charities operate – for example, that some appear to have unacceptably high fundraising costs. Andrew Passey argues that this tension can be resolved and that, where it is, the rewards may be high. Stephen Lee suggests that aggressive marketing techniques used in the 1970s and 1980s may have been counter-productive in terms of creating long-term donor relationships and generating donor satisfaction and trust. Following this, Stephen Pidgeon calls for new charity relationships with donors and argues that charities should replace traditional marketing techniques to donors with the communication of a vision. Finally, the need for a clear understanding of changing donor profiles and new donor relationships is explored by Cathy Pharoah.

A discussion of causes or giving mechanisms will not, however, provide a complete picture of why people give to charity. This elusive topic, which attracts as many opinions as it does research studies, is explored in two chapters by Catherine Walker and Adrian Sargeant. In Chapter 7, Catherine Walker provides an original review of research into motivations for giving, and illustrates the multi-faceted nature of the decision to give with a holistic model of the potential influences. Adrian Sargeant follows this, in Chapter 8, with a more specific review of the research on how marketing and fundraising factors influence the individual in giving.

In the final chapters, a number of authors paint some visions for the future development of giving. In Chapter 9, Richard Fries discusses the need for a legal framework that will re-inspire public trust and confidence in charities while having the flexibility to to allow the definition of charity to evolve in line with changing social contexts and new government expectations of the non-profit sector. David Wickert throws a spotlight on the new opportunities for global action and fundraising. Sarah Hughes speculates on the role of the new media in shaping future donor relationships. John Kingston argues powerfully that charities will only re-engage donors if they substitute the marketing of products with clear re-statements of their visions for change and of the respective roles for themselves and their donors in achieving these visions. Directly following this, Barry Knight pulls together a number of the threads running throughout the book and argues that the twenty-first century will need to see traditional notions of charity replaced by notions of social investment in a future in which the common interests of the different sectors of society – wealthy, excluded, local and global – form a joint agenda for voluntary action.

In the end-note, Chapter 10, the editors of the book summarise the main messages that emerge from the various papers, and explore their implications in terms of policy, research and practice.

Charitable giving is a much more complex topic than many realise and it has received remarkably little study. There is scant understanding of its strength and persistence in Britain in spite of changing social values; nor has there been any assessment of its importance as a statement of values today. The material in this book attempts to convey some of this complexity. It does not aim at any 'grand theory' on giving, but stakes out the territory and the issues that pre-occupy those engaged in promoting individuals to give. In providing information on the state of individual giving to charities today, it aims to make an important contribution to current efforts to renew and invigorate the role of philanthropy in public life in the twenty-first century.

THE EVOLUTION OF CHARITABLE GIVING
Redmond Mullin

EVERYBODY GIVES

It seems that everyone gives and has given and that it was always so. This is the point of the legend, re-cycled for the gospels from Jewish tradition, of the 'widow's mite': Jesus in this story saw her give two coins (worth one sixty-fourth of a labourer's daily wage) and said that she had given more than anyone else, because she had given all she had.

Within the long history of giving there are recurrent themes – such as the generosity of the poor, as illustrated in the legend of the widow – which are as much a part of charity today as of the past. This chapter traces the emergence of notions about charity over time, providing a backdrop to the picture of charitable giving today sketched out in the rest of the book and identifying themes: the persistence of giving and its possibly instinctive or genetic origin, the way giving behaviour so often reflects social expectations in communities, the uneven relationship between what people give and what they can afford, the varying degrees of altruism in the making of a gift, the varying purposes for gifts, and the powerful role of appeals and fundraisers throughout time. As indicated already, the story will begin with the potentially immeasurable or limitless quality in giving.

The mites of the poor

It is difficult to uncover the altruism of the poor. In desperate situations, the destitute have helped each other as best they could. A record of sixteenth-century tin mining in the West Country says that the charity of the marginally better-off miners is 'so great that if one or two or three or else poor men sit among them having neither bread drink or other repast, there is none among them all the rest but will distribute at least the largest sort with the poor work fellowes that have nothing, so that in the end this poor man having nothing to relieve him at work shall in the end be better furnished of bread butter cheese beef pork and bacon, than all the riches sort'. A study of gifts in sixteenth-century France shows food to have been the principal form of charity to the poor from the less poor (Davis, 2000). The migrant shepherd Pierre Maury, early in the fourteenth century, commented: 'If we have but one farthing, we must share it with our poor brothers'. In the twelfth century, Maurice de Sully said that Notre-Dame had been built with the gifts of old women (Mollat, 1986).

De Sully's story, like the parable of the widow's mite, is making a moral not an economic point. However, there is evidence that the poorest in society have contributed both to great enterprises such as public works or building a cathedral and also to the relief of poverty. They are most likely to have done this through collecting boxes, which have always been instruments for popular fundraising. The widow in the gospel story probably dropped her coins into one of the 13 trumpet-shaped collecting boxes placed around the walls of the women's court in the temple. Poor visitors to the poor patients in a fifteenth-century Paris hospital put their gifts into two collecting boxes. Out of 940 coins, 500 were of the lowest denominations. These were the mites of the poor (Mollat, 1986).

Patterns of giving

Direct, local, small-scale mutual support can have only limited effectiveness in dealing with large-scale poverty or in funding capital enterprises. Outside the kinds of limited interpersonal support mentioned above, the patterns of giving have been mixed. By the fourth century BC, the Greeks had distinguished between public subscriptions aimed at the mass of citizens (*epidoseis*) and the rich donors (*euergetai*). There could be conscious expression of community in this, bonding all citizens within a single fundraising drive. An upper limit might be set for an *epidoseis,* to encourage all citizens to give. Sometimes the launch of a public subscription was intended to leverage more spectacular gifts from the rich; although another intention could be to prevent the funding of an enterprise by a single rich man, or by a small group of the rich (Veyne, 1990). Gifts give power.

This pattern of support has been common ever since for certain enterprises: a mass of small gifts, but with clinching major donations from one or more rich individuals. This was the pattern of funding for the cathedrals of Milan, Troyes and other medieval cities.[1] It is the pattern of support seen during the middle ages and the Renaissance for hospitals, some public works and poor relief, as these examples illustrate:

- Duccio's great altarpiece, the *Maesta,* for the cathedral in Sienna was an undertaking by the citizens, not by the cathedral chapter. On its installation in June 1311, on the eve of the feast of the Assumption, every member of the congregation went up to the high altar, giving the best wax candle they could afford (Kempers, 1995).

- A thirteenth-century hospital in Cambridge was funded by townsfolk and villagers; by 'burgesses, modest knights and substantial peasants' (Rubin, 1997).

- During a period ending with the Reformation in protestant lands, a common way in which people came together for pious reasons as well as for philanthropy and public works was through membership of a fraternity or guild. Statutes for a guild formed to act a play on the Lord's Prayer yearly in York said: 'Vain is the gathering of the faithful unless some work of kindliness is done' (Smith, 1870).

- Mobilised by fear of the plague to seek protection from the Virgin, the Fraternita di Santa Maria della Misericordia in Arezzo had a membership of about 1,700 (equivalent to most of Arezzo's adult population) by about 1300. This membership ranged from 'feudal nobility and patricians to artisans, servants and even some laborers', although the officers were 'drawn from the wealthy mercantile elite'. The fraternity was committed to helping the sick and poor and was also a patron of the arts.

This form of activity meant that, through the collectivity of their relatively small subscriptions, ordinary citizens could help those in need and participate in commissioning important works, including

---

[1] *For example, Bishop Stapledon's gift of 1,000 marks in 1325, just before his murder, secured the completion of Exeter Cathedral's nave under his successor, Grandisson.*

paintings and buildings (Wilch and Ahl, 2000). And yet, despite the widespread phenomenon of giving, history shows that it is the great patrons who are remembered, their names sculpted on buildings.

WHAT DO PEOPLE GIVE TO?

Charitable giving has always gone to a diversity of causes. The Greeks' *epidoseis* and *euergetai* could be for city defences, civic buildings or poor relief. In the middle ages, causeways and bridges were equivalently treated as 'charitable' with care for the poor and sick, the provision of dowries, ransoms or education. Today there is a tendency to designate grants to welfare causes 'charitable', and those for the arts or education 'philanthropic'. Historically at least, this is a false distinction, and it fails to reflect the behaviour and perceptions of many donors. The same people gave from the same resources for roads or public buildings or dowries or artworks, as did for poor relief.

Over time, certain of the objects for giving have changed. Cicero, a few decades before the start of the Christian era, seems to have seen 'charity' as a transfer between peers, in favour of those suffering from hard times. These were the 'worthy poor' (*De Officiis* II, ix, V p 55). Seneca, born about the same time as Jesus, distinguished between great public works, which should be glorious, and help to the poor, which should be secret (*De Beneficiis* II, p 64). Cicero favoured private gifts for walls, docks, harbours, aqueducts; was doubtful about funding for theatres, colonnades and new temples; and criticised as vanity sponsorship of banquets, games, wild beast fights, and gladiatorial shows (*De Officiis* II, xvii).

Categories promoted for individual giving during the middle ages and Renaissance, with their Christian inspiration, were more sympathetic and more committed to the poor. They still, however, included public works (such as bridges, causeways, sea defences), always favoured churches, cathedrals and monasteries; and included magnificent civic buildings and works of art. Education and the provision of healthcare in hostels or hospitals were equally favoured. That extension of 'the seven works of mercy', promoted by preachers and by fundraisers, was enshrined in the heads of charity we inherit from the 1601 *Charitable Uses Act* (Wealth 113).[2]

WHY DO PEOPLE GIVE?

Culture and religion give reason enough for many people to give, at least modestly. Christian and Jewish teachings urge believers to give to all who ask, making small alms non-judgemental. There may be genetic advantages for some species in altruism, of which charitable giving is an aspect. The main concern in this chapter is with larger transactions, where judgement may be more closely engaged.

Seneca argued: remove sound judgement from charity and it is not charity (*De Beneficiis*, I, ii, pp 8–9). He was one of a series of writers on charity who wanted there to be order and discipline in giving. This was promoted by Rufinus in the twelfth century as 'ordered charity' (*caritas ordinata*): after God you should prefer parents, then children, then servants; and after these the most needy and humbler petitioners for funds, rather than sturdy beggars (*Summa Elegantius*, Rubin, 1997). Dostoevsky declared 'Compassion has been outlawed by science' at roughly the same time as, in England, Charles Stewart Loch of the Charity Organisation Society was intending by 1875 to discipline the life of the people by 'a nobler, more devoted, more scientific religious charity' (Woodroofe, 1974).

Early theories of giving

The discussions of reasons why and how people should give are ancient and continuous. Ignoring petty alms, Aristotle (384–322 BC) distinguishes in *Nichomachean Ethics* between 'liberality' (which is concerned with significant material support for the needy), 'prodigality' (which is a vulgar imprudent scattering of sums to anyone indiscriminately') and 'lordliness' or 'magnificence' (which is concerned with spectacular public expenditure and significant matters

---

[2]   *These seven works of mercy are defined by John Gaytring in 1357 (York Medieval Texts, 1972): '… the first is to feed them that are hungry. The second is to give them drink that are thirsty. The third is for to clothe them that are clotheless or naked. The fourth is to harbour those that are homeless. The fifth is to visit them that lie in sickness. The sixth is for to help characters that lie in prison. The seventh is to bury dead men who need this. These are the seven bodily deeds of mercy that every man ought to do that might do them.'*

of state) (*Nichomachean Ethics* II, vii; IV, ii & iii; VIII, xiii). Aristotle's 'magnificence' was explicitly promoted in Renaissance Italy, and it was in this sense that Lorenzo de Medici was 'Magnificent'. Alberti in *Ten Books of Architecture* (1485) writes: 'Men of public spirits approve and rejoice when you have raised a fine wall or Portico and adorned it with Portals, columns and a handsome roof, knowing you have thereby not only served yourself, but them too, having by this generous use of your wealth, gained a great Honour to yourself, your family, your Descendants and your City' (*De Re Aedificatoria,* Preface).

That comment concerned great works and conspicuous private palaces, intended to adorn the city, for glory and for public benefit. The overlapping of motives and persuasion is also illustrated by Alberti, where he is dealing with the hospitals or hostels being built at that time: 'And by this Means these poore wretches did not wander about begging Relief, perhaps in vain, and the City was not offended by miserable and filthy objects' (English governments threatening to hose night-sleepers off the Strand would sympathise with this). Those 'Means' were 'noble Hospitals, built at vast expense; where as well Strangers as Natives, are furnished plentifully with all Manner of Necessities for their Cure'.

Thomas Aquinas (1224–1274), in his analysis of liberality, pity and benevolence, and justice, based large parts of his arguments on Aristotle, though his argument was Christian. There is no suggestion in what he writes that charity consists in exchanges between more- and less-fortunate peers. Nor is the concept of 'liberality', transformed in this Christian context, confined to the rich: 'Nothing prevents some good people, although they are poor, from liberality'. Aquinas distinguishes between justice, pity and benevolence: the gift from pity and benevolence comes from feeling for the beneficiary, so is an act of charity or friendship; liberality will benefit strangers as well as acquaintances; justice differs from liberality, 'because justice delivers to the other what is his; liberality delivers what belongs to the donor' (*Summa Theologica,* IIa, IIae, Quaest CXVII). Taken to extremes, all giving was deemed as a function of justice; a tract, written by a British gentleman in Sicily about 410 AD, said: 'Some people are poor because others own too much. Remove the rich and you will find no poor … A few rich people are the reason why there are so many poor' (*De Divitiis,* attributed to Pelagius in *Patrologiae Cursus Completus, series Latina, supplementum*).

Public and religious pressure to give

The common teaching was more moderate than that; but there was persuasive doctrine to give substance to the exhortations for charity. Preaching and indoctrination were underpinned with parish and fraternity structures, both creating strong social expectations that support would be given to approved causes, proportionately by all members of society. This was systematically structured in Jewish societies dispersed across Europe, perhaps particularly in more organised communities such as those in seventeenth-century Poland. But the expectation of conformity in major public appeals was much more ancient than that. In the second great drive for voluntary public subscriptions in Athens, Demosthenes (d 413 BC) attacked a prominent politician for giving only 300 drachmas, less than that given by a well-known Cretan: 'Why, you incorrigible knave … you never came forward and put your name down for a farthing' (Veyne, 1990). How could any of those citizens of Sienna not have contributed, at least a poor candle? And in the great appeal for the Cathedral in Milan, about 1386, where there were major gift fundraising with the court, participation by every guild and fraternity, street collections, jumble sales, how could anyone have dared abstain (Mullin, 1984)?

Early tax reliefs

There were external inducements for giving. In the Greek and Roman worlds, huge gifts by the rich could pre-empt huger tax demands; temples, hostels and other institutions were given tax reliefs; there were charitable trusts or foundations. Responsibility for distributing corn to the poor was, under Constantine, transferred from pagan priests to Christian bishops. One reason for the increasing power of the Christian church within the Roman Empire from the fourth century onwards was that it was the pacifier of the frightening urban mobs, its functions reinforced by their new roles as distributors of state doles (Brown, 1992).

Indulgences – a particularly effective inducement to give

From the time that Urban II launched the first crusade in 1095 until Martin Luther's rejection of the fraud in 1517, indulgences functioned as the most effective fundraising instruments ever invented. They either exploited very private self-interest, or harnessed the vulnerabilities of the poor to such self-interest. The idea behind this brilliant fundraising device was simple: if you confessed your sins to a priest, he would give you a penance; assuming you were not already a saint, you would after death be put in an intermediate place between heaven and hell, where you would be agonisingly purged of any punishment remaining from your sins; the length of those punishments was defined in days and years; when your time was served, you were fit to go to heaven. By buying indulgences on certain sacred feasts or at designated holy places, you could reduce those years of punishment. You might achieve the same result by giving relief to poor people who, as your 'bedesmen', would pray for your soul after death. (You could not be bought out of hell.) Those indulgences attached to all the objects considered so far in this chapter: churches, cathedrals, hospitals, bridges, roads, other good works. They were spectacularly effective: in June 1390, the Milan Cathedral fabric fund raised 2,398 lire; in June 1391, with a Jubilee indulgence, it raised 24,858 lire. Donors were buying fast-track promotion in personal salvation, which was more motivating than any tax concession, and could in itself be a sufficient motivation for giving.

Professional fundraisers were involved, alongside priests, in the sale of indulgences. When and where protestantism eliminated this trade, fundraisers still needed to be deployed to bring in gifts needed for an appeal. Henry VIII, in his Beggar's Act of 1536, established a sophisticated replacement for the sale of indulgences. The argument was to be delivered on a specific day by priest from pulpit; the sermon was to be followed by a visitation by church elders to every household; and alms were to be given only through official boxes. This was part of an attempt across Europe to regulate charity and reduce mendicancy. The beneficiaries were to cover the usual categories: 'poor, needy, sick, sore and indigent persons' and to set the sturdy poor in work (Tanner, 1930). The social pressure to respond must have been overwhelming.

From Victorian charity to giving today

A review of some aspects of individual giving in the twentieth century must start in the nineteenth century. At the top of the giving scale, the pace and principles were set by nineteenth-century rich businessmen who spanned their turn of centuries. John Davidson Rockefeller, who started tithing at Sunday School, and Israel Seiff (who said: 'Justice is the condition in which men help each other. This idea is the essence of being a Jew'), like the Quakers George Cadbury and Joseph Rowntree, were motivated by religion. Henry Wellcome, who founded one of the world's richest foundations, said at 21 that he intended to be rich to fund medical research for the glory of God and the good of mankind. Andrew Carnegie was as philanthropic, but his *Gospel of Wealth* (1889) makes this a social not a religious obligation: 'The man who dies rich dies disgraced.' The Laings, Wates and the old Quakers have carried that religious motivation across the twentieth into the twenty-first century; but the motivations of many present-day major donors are philanthropic, humanist, secular.

The role of tax reliefs

Before and after the introduction of income tax in England in 1799, fiscal inducements for giving were opportunistic. Like mortgage and savings relief, they have always reflected the kinds of behaviour governments have favoured at different periods. In the 1920s, the Rathbones, a great Liverpool philanthropic family, noted that, if someone alienated taxed income on another's behalf, tax would be levied at the rate appropriate for the recipient. If the recipient was a charity, exempt from tax, then a full rebate should be due. This was of course alarming for the treasury, who variously limited the rebates a charity could claim and, eventually, the tax reductions from which a donor could benefit. This was the charitable covenant system. The system in the USA, by contrast, has principally been based on the tax deduction. Regulations for the deduction have varied federally and between states but they have been essentially consistent: make a gift from taxed income or assets to an organisation recognised by the Internal Revenue Service (IRS) as not-for-profit and there will be a proportionate reduction in your tax liability. Covenant, Gift Aid and deduction have reduced the costs of giving. A recent study, drawing on previous research and also on common sense, concludes that taxes do not 'cause people to make contributions, only that the existence of taxes and the associated deduction causes people to give more than they would have otherwise' (Clotfelter, 1980).

New conceptions of altruism itself

Recent analysis of altruism has been influenced by three new strands in thought. One is based on arguments derived from evolutionary theory within socio-biology. E O Wilson (1978 and 1992) distinguishes 'hard-core' altruism, on the one hand – which works beyond expectations of social reward or punishment and which 'is likely to have evolved through kin selection or natural selection operating on entire, competing family or tribal units' – and 'soft-core' altruism on the other, which 'expects reciprocation from society for himself or his closest relatives' and which 'can be expected to have evolved primarily by selection of individuals and to be deeply influenced by the vagaries of cultural evolution'. W D Hamilton (1996) dissolved the distinction between nepotistic and reciprocal altruism: 'But once positive selection supervenes the resemblance between the two situations fades: reciprocal altruism of the kind described is less purely altruistic'. A second strand is philosophical: for example, Thomas Nagel (1970) argues that altruism depends, not on love, 'but on a presumably universal recognition of the reality of other persons'. A third strand, finally, sees philanthropy as the exercise of bourgeois power (most typically in the work of Marx) or as a concatenation of systems for the exercise of control (as described by Foucault), both imposing the will of influential minorities on majorities. These ideas are not explored here, but introduced to illustrate the challenges of defining charity in changing social contexts.

Since 1945, after the establishment of the Welfare State, there have from time to time been tendencies to marginalise charities and to belittle charitable giving. Frank Prochaska notes that Gordon Brown's drive to reinvigorate charitable service '… brings to mind working-class traditions of charity, which were once a bulwark of welfare. Those traditions were largely discarded by twentieth-century collectivists, for whom the word charity became an offensive conceit, associated with hierarchical values and unfashionable pieties' (British

Academy lecture February 8th, 2001; *Times Literary Supplement* Feb 9th). Charities have not been marginalised and, as essential organs of civic society, offer alternatives and challenges to the state, sustaining independent values against centralising pressures for conformity. The expansion of the charity universe has been made possible and sustained through gifts from companies and the more institutional trusts, with some encouragement and support from governments; but for most charities, the main support has come from individuals.

MODERN FUNDRAISING

Before the late 1940s, most overseas aid from England had been for and through Church of England missions. For example, the Society for the Propagation of the Gospels (SPG) was described as 'the first Christian body to occupy Swaziland', and its aim was the 'taming and refining [of the native races] into a nobler, purer manhood' (Mullin, 1984). Overseas aid as we know it developed much later: Save the Children was established in 1919, and the Oxford Committee for Famine Relief, later known as Oxfam, was formed in 1942. Impetus was given to such third-world agencies by World Refugee Year in 1958 (Whitaker, 1983).

These and other welfare organisations have developed a range of techniques for popular fundraising. They have recruited large numbers of regular supporters, expanding a fundraising method seen in ancient Greece, Fraternities of the Fabric in the middle ages and in the lists of regular subscribers initiated by the Society for the Promotion of Christian Knowledge (SPCK) in 1698 and SPG in 1701. Recent refinements have included direct-marketing techniques (foreshadowed by John Bellers' 1696 direct mail appeal for Saffron Walden school), advertising, telephone marketing and experiments with the internet. Such popular fundraising has been boosted by television, for example during the Ethiopian famine (though with the worry that aid reduces when the cameras withdraw), by telethons and by such exercises as Children in Need and Comic Relief.

There were major boosts of other kinds. In the late 1980s, the universities of Oxford and Cambridge each mounted appeals for more than £250 million, unprecedented at the time for England. These secured high levels of alumni support and also attracted a number of multi-million-pound gifts. In 1984, NSPCC launched its Centenary appeal, combining the full range of techniques for national and regional fundraising, from major gifts to mass marketing and events, and raising a then unprecedented £15 million. This was used as a model for Great Ormond Street's successful Wishing Well appeal.

The biggest gifts from rich people over the last fifty years have gone to universities, museums, galleries and cultural organisations, such as the Royal Opera House. The picture is the same in the USA for gifts above £5 million: 'Medical research and higher education dominated this giving ... Of the remaining contributions, cultural organisations garnered the largest share ... followed by private foundations' (Clotfelter, 1980). Even United Way, an outstanding popular fundraising body in the USA, has depended on big gifts for its expansion (*The Chronicle of Philanthropy*, August 26, 1999). In 2000, NSPCC launched its FULL STOP Appeal, the first time a welfare charity in Britain had attempted to secure the very major sums attracted for higher education and the arts. This ambitious campaign for the protection of children may become a new landmark.

While these great enterprises and achievements were taking place, there had been other changes in the fundraising world. In Britain, the Institute of Charity Fundraising Managers (ICFM) was founded to improve the qualities and reputations of fundraisers through the establishment of standards in each main fundraising discipline, and through education and training. At the same time, university courses have multiplied in fundraising and charity management, some co-operating with ICFM, and professional qualifications have been established.

New wealth

Meanwhile, over more than twenty years, the wealth profile of Britain has been changing. There are many more people who are seriously rich. Stuart Wheeler provides a useful illustration of the adjective 'rich': 'Quite frankly, since you're above, I don't know, £20 million, whether you have another five million doesn't affect your standard of living at all'. Many such newly rich people are making gifts, often in millions and sometimes in tens of millions. They do this for all the ancient reasons: from altruism, to affirm a position in society, to mix with the influential and fashionable, even to win honours. They do not differ in any significant ways from the great philanthropists of classical, renaissance or other periods. And their generous gifts are needed for the achievement of great charitable and cultural goals.

There is a new, intermediate group of prospects, who are not rich, but who have significantly greater means than the majority, including the well-salaried. These are people earning over, say, £250,000 yearly, and who need to be targeted in special ways. First proposals for this new segment of possible donors were designed some years ago, and strategies proposed for their development are delivering individual sums between £100,000 and £1 million (Mullin, 2001). Like the rich, this new affluent group can be motivated to give beyond levels they believed they could achieve, or to which they had been invited to achieve.

Throughout the 1990s, both Conservative and Labour administrations have improved the tax environment for donors from top to bottom of the scale for giving. The regime for giving in the UK today matches the USA, even including the concessions on shares recently promoted by billionaires on the US West Coast. And yet, as later chapters in this book show, donors do not give because of the tax concessions by themselves. Only briefly in the USA, and for the very rich, was a net benefit for donors possible from giving. Motivations are more fully explored in later chapters: people give because this is part of their culture, because giving sustains the kind of society or community in which they want to live; they give, sometimes, for social gain, but also, once persuaded, from a less-considered instinct for generosity.

Those wishing to drill the well of new private wealth for a new era of philanthropy can learn much from the experience of the past, whose main messages may be summed up as follows:

- All gifts contain an element of altruism, although altruism is not always present to the same degree in all givers.
- To give is natural to virtually everyone; some altruism appears to be instinctual, and may be part of our genetic inheritance.
- Personal gains might include salvation, assertion of a place in

society, public display of wealth, a search for honour or public glory.

- People give for very different purposes, which may reflect the needs of society at any time – they may wish to fund alternative ways of providing for need.
- Gifts consequently have at times funded civil works, art works, ransoms and dowries, as well as the familiar objects of British charity, such as the relief of poverty.
- Gifts are made for different types of beneficiary, and donors are selective when they give.
- Some givers donate to a number of different causes, embracing, for example, education and arts as well as welfare and poor relief.
- External inducements have often played a role in giving – there have always been appeals and fundraisers of various kinds to secure the funds needed, and donors have often been rewarded through public glory or tax benefits for themselves or their chosen recipients.

In the past, as now, giving to charity has always been a complex affair: there is as much diversity as similarity between individuals in their motivations for giving and their preferences for giving.

References

Brown P (1992) *Power and Persuasion in Late Antiquity*. University of Wisconsin Press.

Clotfelter C (1980) 'Tax Incentives and Charitable Giving: evidence from a panel of taxpayers', *Journal of Public Economics*, **13**: 319–40.

Hamilton W D (1996) *Narrow Roads of Gene Land*. Oxford: Spektrum.

Kempers T da Costa (1995) *Court, Cloister and City: the art and culture of Central Europe 1450–1800*. London: Weidenfeld & Nicolson.

Mollat M (1986) *The Poor in the Middle Ages*. Yale University Press.

Mullin R (1984) *The Wealth of Christians*. Ossening: Orbis.

Mullin R (2001) 'The Prosperous: a new segment for fundraising', *Professional Fundraising*, March 2001.

Nagel T (1970) *The Possibility of Altruism*. Princeton University Press.

Rubin M (1997) *Charity and Community in Medieval Cambridge*. Cambridge University Press.

Smith T (1870) *English Gilds*. Early English Text Society.

Tanner J R (1930) *Tudor Constitutional Documents 1485–1603*. Cambridge University Press.

Veyne P (1990) *Bread and Circuses*. London: Allen Lane Penguin Press.

Whitaker B (1983) *A Bridge of People: a personal view of Oxfam's first forty years*. London: Heinemann.

Wilch B and Ahl D C (eds) (2000) *Confraternities and the Visual Arts in Renaissance Italy*. Cambridge University Press.

Wilson E O (1978) *On Human Nature*. Harvard University Press.

Wilson E O (1992) *The Diversity of Life*. London: Allen Lane Penguin Press.

Woodroofe K (1974) *From Charity to Social Work in England and the United States*. London: Routledge and Kegan Paul.

HOW MUCH DO PEOPLE GIVE TO CHARITY, AND WHO ARE THE DONORS?

Cathy Pharoah

MEASURING GIVING – A COMPLICATED PROCESS

Why does it matter how much we give? What do levels of giving mean? Certainly charitable giving is of huge significance to charities – for the many major fundraising charities, it constitutes anything from 30 per cent to 90 per cent of income. A majority of the public gives to charity, with over two-thirds donating money each year, but public giving has come to be seen as much more than an indicator of charities' financial health. Many see it as a key social indicator, with a wider significance for questions such as:

- How generous or selfish is our society today?
- Is government policy crowding out public spiritedness?
- How great is the squeeze on personal finances?
- Are charities losing public faith and trust?
- Are levels of social capital (the relationships of trust and reciprocity that bind society together) declining?

So the question of how much the public gives to charities, and whether this is changing, is one of some importance. Annoyingly, there is no simple answer.

Charities raise funds from the public in a multitude of ways, which means that measuring this diverse set of activities is highly complex. Most progress in this area stems from the voluntary sector itself, in the shape of surveys commissioned by CAF (Charities Aid Foundation) and NCVO (National Council for Voluntary Organisations). Government surveys too have captured data on giving, but only as part of much broader measures of family expenditure. There is also a range of government administrative data, such as income tax recovered by charities on particular types of donation, and the annual value of legacies to charity in individual wills. A fully comprehensive estimate of giving by the general public needs to take account of this multitude of sources; however, it is not as simple as adding them all together to come up with a final figure.

This is often a cause of great frustration – particularly among a public now well used to a huge amount of published data on public- and private-sector performance. And this problem cannot be easily resolved – at least, not without significantly greater government or charity investment in the collection of data than there has been in the past. Any overall comprehensive estimate, therefore, is a composite from different sources.

The complications of gathering statistics on charitable giving include:

- which types of charity to include (sports clubs, political parties, non-profit hospitals, public schools?);
- which countries to include (Great Britain, UK, England and Wales?);
- how to generate appropriate estimates for the annual giving of the population from small sample surveys of generally small gifts;
- how to ensure that all types of giving are adequately included (for example, is giving to a local school or playgroup a charitable gift?);
- how to capture those highly valued but highly elusive major gifts (how many doors must be knocked on, or telephone calls made, to find a reasonable sample of people who donate £20,000 a year or more?);
- how to track accurately levels of legacy giving at any one point in time – gifts that are out of normal daily time and place.

The different surveys available take different approaches to these issues and they cover varying periods of time. Any figure for giving is at best a composite from the different sources. In fact, the challenge of whether economics provides any appropriate way of valuing our gifts pales into insignificance beside the challenge of actually obtaining accurate economic estimates. With these factors in mind, what is presented below should be seen as a range of 'working estimates'. Different surveys are appropriate for answering different types of question – the guiding principle for anyone seeking data is to choose the survey or source best suited to individual purpose.

AN ESTIMATE FOR TOTAL GIVING

The key source of information on individual giving is the annual surveys of individual giving commissioned initially by CAF from Professor Peter Halfpenny at Manchester University, who carried out seven annual surveys until 1993. In 1994, NCVO placed a sub-set of questions from this survey in a National Opinion Poll (NOP) Omnibus Survey, and these NCVO/NOP surveys of individual giving have been carried out regularly since then.[1] In 1999, 2000 and 2001, CAF and the Inland Revenue (IR) joined with NCVO/NOP to explore tax-effective giving in more detail.[2] Various reports that draw on this body of survey work have been published; some of these publications are specified in this book.

The cost of these surveys is almost entirely borne by the charity sector, and they are carried out on a voluntary basis. The surveys are the best regular source of information on the general public's individual gifts to charities: they collect detail on a wide range of methods – from street collections and direct mail appeals to charity shopping and long-term tax-effective covenants.

Because of the difficulty of tracking those high-value but rare donors in the population, as noted above, these surveys do not capture a fully representative sample of larger gifts – for example, they do not measure legacies. Nonetheless they are an immensely valuable source of information and provide the basis for an overall comprehensive estimate for individual giving, which can be built up using data from different sources:

* the NCVO/NOP 2001 individual giving survey provides an estimate for total individual giving of approximately £5.7 billion per annum:

* a rough estimate of an additional £400 million needs to be added

---

[1] *These surveys are referred to in this book as 'NCVO/NOP', followed by the relevant year.*
[2] *This work is referred to in this book as 'CAF/IR/NCVO', followed by the relevant year.*

to this to take account of its under-representation of bigger gifts, particularly what is called 'tax-effective' or 'planned' giving, that is individual gifts made through covenants or Gift Aid;

• income tax on individual gifts through covenants and Gift Aid repaid to charities by the Inland Revenue amounts to a further £425 million.

This yields an estimate for the total amount given by the public of £6.1 billion per year. A further £1.5 billion is donated per annum in the form of legacies (Smee & Ford, unpublished estimates).[3]

ARE WE GIVING MORE OR LESS TO CHARITIES OVER TIME?

If levels of giving to charity are an important social as well as economic indicator, the question of whether public giving is increasing or decreasing is an important one to answer. Clearly, if it is difficult to get a single annual estimate for giving, then tracking change is also fairly problematic. Different surveys have indicated different trends, and it is worth looking at each of these separately before coming to some overall conclusion.

Indications of decline

The individual giving surveys again provide the starting point. They have generally repeated the same questions in the same way over time, and, on the basis of this data, NCVO has provided annual monitoring of trends since it took over the survey in 1994. NCVO has argued that trends throughout the 1990s point to an overall fall in levels of charitable giving; there have been signs of a small pick-up from 1998, but no return to the levels of 1993 (see Table 3.1).

To determine trends fully, however, it is necessary also to consider evidence from other sources, particularly those that give fuller data on the larger gifts. These suggest that some types of giving are

---

[3] *A complication is that this legacy figure includes bequests to many institutions such as universities, which the public might not think of as charities and which they would not include when asked about their giving in the individual giving surveys.*

Table 3.1   The annual amount given by adults to charities, 1993–2000 (£)

Year	Average annual giving per adult[1] (1995 prices) (£)
1993	10.71
1995[2]	9.95
1996	8.48
1997	8.09
1998	8.25
1999	9.76
2000	10.35

Source NCVO (2001).

[1]All adults in the population (not just givers).
[2]No annual figure is available for 1994.

increasing. In addition to this, the NCVO/NOP surveys do not include legacies, and these can be added into their estimates.

Indications of growth

Legacies

Throughout the mid- to late-1980s, legacy income to charities increased enormously, reflecting increasing inter-generational transfers of property, the huge boom in house prices in certain areas of the country, and a booming stock market. This growth rate was not sustainable in the 1990s, and, in view of declining legacy income, a number of charities commissioned NCVO/Henley to model future trends. Their model suggested that legacy income would continue to decline as pressures to pay for care in old age claimed estates. In fact, the 1990s have seen a continuing growth in legacy income, but at a significantly slower rate than during the 1980s. Between 1994/95 and 1997/98, the value of net estates bequeathed to charities grew from £628 million to £854.6 million, although this cannot be used as an absolute indicator of the amount granted to charities because of time lags in notification.[4] Table 3.2 shows the growth in the value of legacies to the top 500 fundraising charities throughout the 1990s.[5] Trends in legacy giving are further discussed in the following chapter.

Table 3.2 Real-terms growth in value of legacies to the top 500 fundraising charities, 1991–99 (%)

1991/92–1992/93	+2
1992/93–1994/95	+5
1994/95–1995/96	−3
1995/96–1996/97	+7
1996/97–1997/98	+14
1997/98–1998/99	+4

Source *Dimensions of the Voluntary Sector*, CAF (1991–2000).

Other tax-effective giving

The majority of the biggest gifts to charity are made 'tax-effectively', and the IR's annual published statistics on levels of tax repaid to charities provide one key source of information on changes in giving to charity. Most of these statistics indicate levels of growth in tax-effective giving that far outstrip inflation. The key issue, therefore, in determining whether overall giving has changed is whether tax-effective giving has added to the total amount given in the more traditional ways, or whether it substitutes for these forms of giving. The interesting question of whether tax reliefs provide incentives to give, and to give more, is discussed in Chapter 5.

Charitable tax reliefs are available on various forms of giving – for example, inheritance tax relief on legacies, and capital gains tax

---

[4] *This book follows the convention of indicating tax years by an oblique stroke (eg, as here, 1994/95) and calendar years by a dash (eg 1994–95).*

[5] *CAF has compiled lists of the top fundraising charities since 1978 from data on income (from voluntary sources, grants and other sources), expenditure and assets supplied by the charities themselves. Since 1993 this list has expanded to include the top 500 fundraising charities. These lists have been published in successive editions of* Dimensions of the Voluntary Sector, *which Cathy Pharoah has edited since 1996.*

relief on gifts of assets. During the 1980s and 1990s two new schemes for giving to charity that carried tax reliefs on income tax were added to the traditional covenants – Gift Aid and payroll giving. The Budget 2000 extended income tax reliefs to gifts of assets. These so-called 'tax-effective' ways of giving are also discussed in detail in Chapter 5.

Covenants These were phased out as tax-effective vehicles for giving in the Budget 2000, largely because they were complicated to administer. They were replaced by Gift Aid. It is difficult to track changes in personal covenant income to charities because the IR statistics do not separate out company and personal covenants. According to IR statistics, net covenant income to charities has grown from £580 million in 1992/93 to £900 million in 1998/99, a growth of 55 per cent. It is possible that personal covenant income to charities today may be worth £740 million, plus tax.[6]

Gift Aid The value of gross gifts made by individuals under the Gift Aid scheme has grown fairly rapidly from £26 million in 1990/91 to £557 million in 1999/2000, and the number of gifts made increased from 9,390 in 1990/91 to 216,600 in 1996/97. Unfortunately, however, complete data are no longer being published by the IR, so it is now difficult to monitor trends for participation.

Payroll giving The value of gross amounts given by individuals through the payroll-giving scheme has grown steadily from £1 million in 1987/88 to £55 million in 2000/01, although about £8 million of this latter figure is due to the Children's Promise scheme, which is principally a one-off effort. The number of employers and employees in the scheme has also grown steadily.

Shares and securities The growth in share owning has resulted in about 29,000 donors who currently give shares to charity, or have sold shares and securities to make a gift. The new income tax reliefs

---

[6] *This figure is an estimate, reached by taking Halfpenny's estimate in 1993 that personal covenants gifted to charities represented about £477 million, 88 per cent of total net covenant income. The estimate of £740 million is based on an assumption that the growth in covenant income represents a steady growth in the personal element. It is possible that the balance between personal and covenant income in the IR total has changed, but there is no data on this. Data on the major fundraising charities shows covenant income to have grown steadily throughout the 1990s (CAF, 1991–2000).*

on gifts of shares and securities will make share giving more attractive, and already some large share gifts have been made, although there is no data as yet.

Family and household gifts to charities

The figures considered so far have looked at gifts either as made by individuals alone, or as taken out of individual incomes. Analysis of the government's annual Family Expenditure Survey (FES), commissioned by CAF from the Institute of Fiscal Studies (IFS), provides a different view of charitable giving. The FES provides information on giving by families or households, and not by individuals. The extent to which charitable decision making is a household or individual decision is discussed in Chapter 7. Clearly, where bigger gifts are concerned and where decisions might be related to overall wealth (as opposed simply to income), an element of joint decision making is likely to be involved.

The FES provides a limited measure of giving, as it excludes charitable purchases such as, for example, buying from charity shops or from Christmas card catalogues. Its great strength is that it provides very long-term data, and that it can relate household charitable giving to other forms of household expenditure. The long-term picture painted by the IFS is one in which the real-terms value of household gifts to charity virtually doubled between 1975 and 1998; however, this was accompanied by a long-term decline in household participation in giving, particularly among younger households. The analysis of the FES also showed the stark contrast in the average amounts given by younger and older age-bands (see Table 3.3).

The NCVO/NOP individual giving surveys have also charted a decline in participation in giving. In other words, although looking at different units of measurement (individual and household), both surveys show the same declining trend in participation.

In contrast to both these sets of data, the IR data indicates a virtually unbroken line of growth of participation in tax-effective giving throughout the 1990s. So what are the true trends in charitable giving in the 1990s?

Table 3.3 Participation in giving and level of contributions by age group of head of household, 1997–98 (FES/IFS)

Age band	Level of weekly giving (£)	Level of participation in giving (%)
20–29	3.11	17.4
30–39	3.14	27.4
40–49	4.89	32.6
50–59	5.06	33.6
60–69	4.36	34.8
70+	5.06	33.8

Giving trends over the last ten years

At the time of the 2000 Budget, whose changes mean that virtually all forms of giving can now be made tax-effective through the new form of Gift Aid, just under half of the money given to charities by the public (43 per cent) was given tax-effectively. Every indicator of tax-effective giving shows that the amount given tax-effectively has grown through the 1990s, and there is some indication that numbers of people participating in tax-effective giving has grown as well. If the estimates for total giving reached in the individual giving surveys for 1993 and 2000 are adjusted to take full account of large tax-effective gifts, and the value of legacies and tax repayments is included, it can be shown that gifts have increased from approximately £6.2 billion in 1993 to 7.6 billion in 2000, a real-terms increase of 6 per cent over this period.

Similar trends can be derived from CAF's continuous annual surveys of the voluntary income of the top 500 fundraising charities. Results from these surveys have shown ongoing growth in charity income from individual giving throughout the 1990s, although, as NCVO research has shown, this growth has mainly benefited the bigger charities.

Table 3.4 shows growth in the voluntary income only, that is, excluding trading and investment income.

Bigger gifts? More donors? More gifts?

What does the pattern of trends in giving outlined above mean for the questions asked at the beginning of this section? The evidence suggests that throughout the 1990s fewer donors made larger and more numerous gifts. These donors may have been particularly attracted to tax-effective methods of giving. A number of factors might underlie such trends: changing techniques of fundraising; the increasing wealth of the top 10 or 20 per cent of people; the value of estates bequeathed to charities, which appreciated enormously in value in the 1980s and 1990s. The element of tax relief that is paid back to the donor might also have had an incentive effect – about £612 million of charitable gifts were made by higher-rate tax payers who received a direct tax relief themselves on their gifts. It is widely argued that the high levels of giving in the USA are related to their tax system, in which charitable tax reliefs are actually returned to donors. This increasingly polarised pattern of giving has implications for the questions posed at the beginning of this chapter about the

Table 3.4 Real-terms growth in value of voluntary income[1] to top 500 fundraising charities, 1991–99 (%)

1991/92–1992/93	+3
1992/93–1994/95	+7
1994/95–1995/96	+1
1995/96–1996/97	+8
1996/97–1997/98	+12
1997/98–1998/99	+3

Source CAF (1991–2000).

[1]CAF's voluntary income figures contain a small amount of both corporate and independent foundation giving; these are not likely to have contributed much to the increase in the rate of change, as foundation giving grows very slowly, and corporate giving has barely increased throughout the 1990s.

generosity of our society, the decline or increase in social capital, and the effects of government policy. Do modern approaches to fundraising actually exclude certain groups in society, such as the less well off or the less tax-literate? These questions are further explored throughout the book.

A lot of give?

The title of this book implies both that there is a lot of giving, but also that there could be more. Do we give a lot, or a little? The figures for charitable giving (in the FES) in relation to other earnings and expenditure provide some interesting perspectives:

- Charitable giving is 1.3 per cent of weekly household expenditure; tobacco is 2 per cent, alcohol is 4 per cent.
- The richest 20 per cent devote 0.7 per cent of their household expenditure to charities.
- The poorest 10 per cent are more generous, devoting 3 per cent of expenditure to charities.
- Charitable giving represents 1 per cent of gross domestic product (GDP).
- Average weekly expenditure on charities is £4.40; on eating out it is £5 per person.

Although some elements of giving, such as legacies and charitable purchases, are excluded from these figures, it is still hard to avoid the conclusion that in general British people as a whole could afford to give considerably more to charity, although some individuals are clearly already very generous. The government's recent measures to promote giving acknowledge the scope to give more, and the Giving Campaign, which is being jointly run and funded by government and the voluntary sector, is aiming to set a new and higher target for giving in the future (the Giving Campaign is described in the Introduction to this book, see p 2).

WHO GIVES TO CHARITIES?

Most surveys of charitable giving show that levels of giving are related directly to income, age, education and occupation. This is true of individual and household giving. The FES also shows that the presence of women and children in the household are important. Both individual-giving surveys and also the FES show that there are regional variations in giving, with the highest levels in the South East.

Analysing data from individual giving surveys in 1998, Passey et al (2000) show that, although around 68 per cent of the population donates to charity, there are marked differences according to demographic characteristics. Seventy per cent of women donate, compared with 61 per cent of men. People in social class AB give more, and more often, than people in social class DE.[7] The 45–54 age group gives the most.

Charitable giving is characterised by the usual 80/20 rule – a small number of people are responsible for a large amount of the giving. Jas (Passey et al, 2000) looks at the difference between those who give over £50 and those who give under £50. It is concluded that the 3 per cent of people who give more than £50 per month contribute over half the total donations.

Results of exploratory research carried out by CAF/IR /NCVO 1999 before the Budget 2000 charitable tax changes illustrate the connection between income and willingness to give. One question asked whether donors would make a gift of £100, £50 or £20 to one charity in one year if this were the only way to get tax back. The results presented in Table 3.5 show how, even at gifts of £20 per year, the numbers on low incomes who said they could afford such gifts are half those on higher incomes. It was such results that persuaded government ultimately to remove all thresholds for charitable gifts made under Gift Aid. The results also show how few people earning over £35,000 per annum felt they would make one-off gifts of £100 or of £50 to charity.

---

[7] *These social class groupings refer to the index developed by the Market Research Society (1993). People are graded principally by their occupation, from A at the top (extremely senior managers and professional people) down to E (all those entirely dependent on the state long-term, unemployed for more than six months and casual workers).*

Table 3.5 Relationship between annual income and willingness to give to charity at certain levels

Average annual household income (£)	Would donate £100+ to one charity in one year (%)	Would donate £50+ to one charity in one year (%)	Would donate £20+ to one charity in one year (%)
2,500–7,500	2	5	14
7,500–<13,500	6	7	27
13,500–<25,000	14	19	32
25,000–<35,000	26	12	30
35,000+	19	19	47

Source CAF/IR/NCVO (1999, unpublished).

Regular giving to charity is considerably less attractive to poorer donors, as Table 3.6 shows.

Table 3.6 Relationship between annual income and regularity of support for charities

Average annual household income (£)	Prefer to give occasionally (%)	Prefer to give regularly (%)	Both (%)
2,500–7,500	62	7	2
7,500–<13,500	52	17	2
13,500–<25,000	55	15	4
25,000–<35,000	53	21	7
35,000+	47	23	12

Source CAF/IR/NCVO (1999, unpublished).

Charity as a 'luxury good' – who gives and how much they give

Turning to giving by households, similar relationships between wealth and characteristics such as education, employment and home

ownership have been shown. The main findings of the analysis of the
FES carried out by the IFS in relation to a number of key
characteristics are summarised here.

Table 3.7 Key characteristics of donor households

Key characteristic	Probability of giving	Effect on levels of giving
Income	For each 10 per cent increase in household income, there is a 1.2 per cent increase in participation in giving.	For every 1 per cent increase in expenditure, there is a 1.1 per cent increase in size of donations.
Age	For every increase of 10 years in the age of the head of the household, there is an increased likelihood of giving of 3 per cent.	For every increase of 10 years in the age of the head of the household, there is a 30 per cent increase in value of donations.
Children	Households with children are 3 per cent more likely to give than those without.	[no information]
Wealth	Home owners are 6 per cent more likely to give than non-home-owners, and the effect of each additional room is to raise the likelihood of giving by 1 per cent.	Home ownership increases size of donations by 14 per cent.
Education	Households where the head has A levels are 5 per cent more likely to give and, where college-educated, 11 per cent more likely to give.	The effect of having A levels is to increase the size of donations by 38 per cent, and the effect of college education is an 80 per cent raise.
Employment status	Households where the head is self-employed are 11 per cent less likely to give; where unemployed, they are 7 per cent less likely to give.	Those not in work are likely to give 20 per cent more than where the head is employed or self-employed.

Source Banks and Tanner (1997).

Education, home ownership, income, wealth, age and spending power are strongly inter-related, and it is difficult to disentangle the effect of one from another. There is considerable evidence that it is the middle-class professional older donor, probably living in the South East, who gives the most to charity. In Chapter 6, detailed descriptions of those donors using tax-effective schemes are given, data that underline even more strongly the difference in the constituencies of those who can give a lot and those who give less to charities. As the IFS has argued, in economic terms charitable giving is a luxury good. The questions for future philanthropy are how far fundraisers will exacerbate the bias to the rich, and whether the concept of 'nice if you can afford it' can be converted into 'essential, because you can afford it'.

GIVING IN ITS DIVERSITY

The surveys reported above do not provide hard information on giving by the black and minority ethnic communities. This lack of data needs to be addressed in future studies. This section highlights some of the available research and emerging issues.

There are some signs that at last attention is beginning to fall on the strong giving traditions within the diverse communities of Britain's population today. Obvious evidence of well-organised and highly successful charitable fundraising among the Asian communities, for example, lies in the many mosques with the associated non-profit social and educational activities they have built in this country. In spite of such powerful illustrations, however, little profile has been given to giving patterns and successful fundraising techniques among black and minority ethnic communities more generally.

This is a great loss, because an understanding of how charity translates from one culture to another and from one country to another, as populations move and emigrate, would reveal much about the heart of philanthropy itself. There are many fascinating issues. Do charitable impulses survive when people leave their country of origin? Are loyalties transferred to new causes in new communities, or are the bonds with former allegiances and cultures actually strengthened? Is new-found wealth directed to former charitable support, or to new causes in the new home country? Another vital question is the extent to which traditions of giving are passed on to successive generations: does this happen, or do different generations or cohorts within immigrant populations develop their own distinct patterns of giving? It would be fascinating to know whether there is something special about charity that makes cultures of giving among immigrant groups any more or less resistant to change than other traditions.

Moving from giving to fundraising, it is important to know the extent to which fundraising techniques in Britain are appropriate for minority communities. In his speech at the Institute of Charity Fundraising Managers' (ICFM) Conference in 2001, Deepak Mahtani, a fundraising consultant, drew attention to some basic issues, describing, for example, how some Hindus may be superstitious about drawing up wills in case it precipitates their demise, and that the role of women, dowries and the older son as heir can affect donor behaviour. He also drew attention to generational differences, saying that while 'the first generation of immigrants focused on surviving, the second is looking to go one step further and be accepted in mainstream society'. There are also broader issues of whether minority communities prefer particular kinds of cause (such as medical causes related to their own health experiences), or whether local and community giving in the main population centres are more appealing than national British giving. Exploring charity in its comparative multicultural context provides an excellent opportunity to find out more about the most important influences on giving.

Many of the minorities who settle in Britain come from countries and regions with powerful cultures and histories of giving. There would be a huge benefit to charities in Britain from understanding and linking into such cultures, both in their traditional and modern-day forms. It is not possible here to describe the long histories of individual giving in its various forms in the different countries and cultures of the world. All the world's great faiths and cultures have promoted the value of voluntarism through philanthropy and charity. In Islam the concepts of *zakat* and *sadaqa* enshrine the giving of money or gifts in kind. In Hinduism the central concept of *daanam* (the act of giving) takes many forms. Sikhism has the concept of *kar seva* (service to each other). Confucian teachings highlight 'humaneness', and there is a long history of private benevolence for public good in China. Jewish concepts of charity have both long religious and secular traditions (Ilchman et al, 1998).

Awareness of the multicultural nature of giving has grown enormously within the USA over the last few years, and for a number of reasons is beginning to emerge in the UK. Successful members of the black and minority ethnic communities themselves have begun to provide greater leadership for giving in general. The Ethnic Minority Foundation (EMF) was established in 2000 under the auspices of the Council of Ethnic Minority Voluntary Sector Organisations (CEMVO), with the aim of building an endowment fund of £100 million to provide a dedicated source of funding for the black voluntary sector. It is particularly intended to stimulate donations from successful business people and other wealthy members of black and minority ethnic communities. The British fundraising profession is also beginning to turn its attention to other successful models and traditions as it seeks to reverse the decline in giving among the general British population. Finally, policy makers are increasingly acknowledging that social inclusion depends on engaging voluntary action from all communities, and that they must build on the activities of the many members of black and minority ethnic communities already heavily engaged in local and community voluntarism.

The multicultural giving research programme of the Center for the Study of Philanthropy at the City University of New York is looking at old-world traditions and how, across time and place, different ethnic and religious groups used gifts of time and money to build non-profit institutions, forge public–private partnerships, promote social and legislative change, and participate in public policy making at local, federal and state levels within the USA. It is not hard to see how many similar stories could be written in Britain.

The influence of culture and identity on giving

An example of the work that needs to be done can be taken from the way in which giving within the Jewish community has been approached, as has been well documented recently by the Institute for Jewish Policy Research (JPR). Research has looked not only at levels of giving, but also at key influences on giving, such as cultural allegiances. It has identified some important issues: for example, people who consider themselves to be more Jewish give twice as much on average as those who define themselves as more British or as equally British and Jewish (a median of £200 annual giving among the former, compared with £100 among the latter). A generational effect was also found, with younger Jewish people much less likely to believe that Jews have a special responsibility to give than those aged over 70. There was a significant relationship between religious outlook and perceived responsibility to give to charity – the more traditional the religious identity, the stronger the belief in a special Jewish responsibility. It was also shown that people who saw themselves as more Jewish were much more likely to donate specifically to Jewish causes in Britain and to Israeli causes than those who saw themselves as British or British/Jewish; they were also much less likely to support general British charities. Within the Jewish community there are strong traditions of giving, with the result that almost one-third of the income of Jewish organisations within Britain is derived from individual donations.

These are extremely important findings, and it would be fascinating to know more about how such patterns play out in other communities. A major reason for the failure to appreciate the strength of giving traditions within Britain's diverse communities has been the tendency among researchers and policy makers over the last decade or so to discount faith-based giving, particularly where linked to specific faith-based causes, as real philanthropy. For example, when Lester Salamon and others set up the International Comparative Non-Profit Sector Research Project in the early 1990s, the first major systematic comparative international account of the voluntary sector, it was decided to exclude giving for religious purposes. Such giving was seen as a non-inclusive and partisan source of voluntary help. The result of this was that at least one country, Italy, decided initially not to take part in the study, because it would exclude the majority of giving in that country, which took place through the Catholic church. Ten years later, the fact that much giving is by faith-based communities through their denominations is being recognised through a growing number of studies of both religious giving and giving by black and minority ethnic communities. Grant makers are under increasing pressure to include faith-based groups among the constituencies they fund.

Developing appropriate tools for measurement

Collecting good information on how much people give depends on understanding the main ways in which they give. Discounting faith-based giving is one factor that would lead to an underestimate of minority giving. Another is the tendency of UK and US surveys of giving to focus only on formal giving to registered charities, and to pay scant attention to more informal giving to friends, family and self-help community groups. Similarly, their focus on absolute amounts rather than the proportion of income given could lead to an under-valuation of charitable giving among black and minority ethnic groups. Absolute amounts given are strongly related to total income, and although there are many wealthy citizens in minority populations, it is still the case that in general there is a consistent income imbalance between black and minority ethnic communities and the white UK and US populations. In the UK, for example, although Chinese and Indian working families average slightly higher earnings than white families, Caribbean and African earnings are significantly lower than white earnings, and Pakistani and Bangladeshi families' earnings are much lower than those of any other group. Turning from earnings to household income, the proportion of families with income below 50 per cent of the national average is higher in every ethnic group than it is among white households (Hills, 1998). Although average incomes in the black communities in the USA are well below the national averages, such communities give more on a percentage basis than others of the same income level. In general, US and UK surveys have shown that poorer people give away a higher proportion of their income, although less in absolute terms (Banks & Tanner, 1997). This could explain why only a small amount of the income of the black and minority ethnic voluntary sector in Britain, unlike Jewish organisations, is derived from individual contributions (although the very existence of the black and minority sector is heavily dependent on other gifts in kind, and on gifts of time and expertise).

Charitable behaviour in the black and minority ethnic communities is likely to prove a rich mine of giving experience and of gifts. Much better information on giving within Britain's diverse communities, collected through techniques sensitive to different traditions of giving, would enable the role and potential of black and minority ethnic communities to be fully appreciated. It would also help develop policies that enable givers in different minority communities to benefit from access to the full range of tax reliefs on gifts that are available.

References

Banks J and Tanner S (1997) *The State of Donation*. London: IFS.

CAF *Dimensions of the Voluntary Sector*, 1991–2000 editions. West Malling: CAF.

Hills J (1998) *Income and Wealth: the latest evidence*. York: Joseph Rowntree Foundation.

Ilchman WF, Katz SN and Queen EL (1998) *Philanthropy in the World's Traditions*. Indiana: Indiana University Press.

NCVO (2001) *Research Quarterly*, Spring. London: NCVO.

Passey A, Hems L and Jas P (2000) *The UK Voluntary Sector Almanac 2000*. London: NCVO.

FUNDRAISING METHODS –
HOW PEOPLE GIVE

There are many different ways in which individual donations can make their way to charity, adding to the myriad of choices a donor faces when deciding to support charity. This chapter will look at the relative success of the different ways in which charities approach people with requests for donations, how different giving mechanisms attract different people, what changes and trends there have been in the cost-effectiveness of different methods over the last few years, and the potential of the internet as a major new way of giving. The chapter will end with a look at legacy fundraising, which is often seen as a rather specialised approach, isolated from mainstream fundraising strategies. Since the discussion of legacies introduces the question of tax-effectiveness in giving mechanisms, it paves the way for the following chapter, which takes a detailed look at the methods of giving that provide income tax reliefs.

HOW THE GENERAL PUBLIC GIVES   Pauline Jas

The information on which this section is based is derived from the NCVO/NOP individual giving surveys. These are face-to-face interviews carried out in people's homes as part of NOP's omnibus survey. Respondents are asked whether they give to charity, how they have given, how much they have given, and to which causes. All questions relate to people's behaviour over the past month, which is considered to be a long enough period to capture what may be infrequent behaviour, but not so long as to jeopardise the reliability of people's memory.

The findings from these surveys do not provide us with an answer to the question of why certain approaches are more successful with some people than with others, because people were not asked why they gave in certain ways, or what their motivations for making gifts were; these issues are, however, explored in more detail by Adrian Sargeant in Chapter 8. However, we can look at how many gifts and how much money people give overall, and then see if the same holds true for different sub-groups within the population. If we then compare the various methods these groups have used to donate money to charity, we can start to understand the relative success of different fundraising approaches.

Basic patterns of giving in the general population are as follows:

• Women give more, and more women give than men.

• The average donations and the number of people giving are closely related to social class – people from class AB give more than people from class C1, who give more than people from class C2, who give more than people from class DE.

• The youngest (16–24) and the oldest (65+) people are less likely to be donors than the groups in the middle (25–64).

(See Table 4.1.)

Table 4.1 Average donation and participation rate for the year 2000, by sex, social class and age

	Participation rate (%)	Average donation (£/month)
Sex		
male	63.5	9.93
female	71.3	10.77
Social class		
AB	79.5	22.63
C1	72.3	11.85
C2	64.8	6.59
DE	58.2	4.65
Age		
16–24	55.0	6.12
25–34	71.9	8.73
35–44	69.5	13.04
45–54	71.7	13.06
55–64	68.9	11.86
65+	65.5	9.24

Breaking down the total amount given into what is given by different groups in the population reveals one factor that stands out as influencing giving: affluence. This is most clear when comparing average donations by social class. The division into classes is based on profession and therefore serves as a reasonable estimate of income. Although it was shown in Chapter 3 that giving as a proportion of total expenditure is higher for people with lower incomes, the absolute values are directly related to income. Economic circumstances are not, however, the only influence on the size of the gift an individual makes, so we will now look at how different people use the various methods of giving.

Frequency of giving, the size of the gift and the method of giving

The total amount of money raised through charitable giving is the result of two factors: the size of the gift and the number of people who give. Within segments of the general population these two tend to be closely related: when a group shows a high propensity to give, their average donation also tends to be higher than in groups where fewer people give. There is no relationship, however, between high use of a method of giving and the size of the gift made by it: there are methods that are used infrequently, but for larger amounts; on the other hand, there are the more common methods, which induce lots of people to give small amounts of money (see Figure 4.1).

It is clear that there are methods of giving which attract a high percentage of givers but provide only a small proportion of the total amount given. These are the 'small change' methods that require a low level of commitment from the donor – the more traditional collections, with a person holding a bucket or rattling a tin.

For those methods – such as buying from a charity shop, setting up a payroll deduction or sponsorship, responding to appeals through advertisements or on television – that require a more active decision, the amount raised (yield), as a proportion of the total amount given, is comparable with the proportion of people using the methods.

For those methods, finally, where donors commit to making regular donations through membership or subscription, the amount raised is an extremely high proportion of the total amount given, even though the percentage of givers using these methods is small. The best example of these is covenants, which attract less than 5 per cent of the population but nearly 15 per cent of the total amount given.[1]

Figure 4.1 Use of giving methods by proportion of population and percentage of average gift (%)

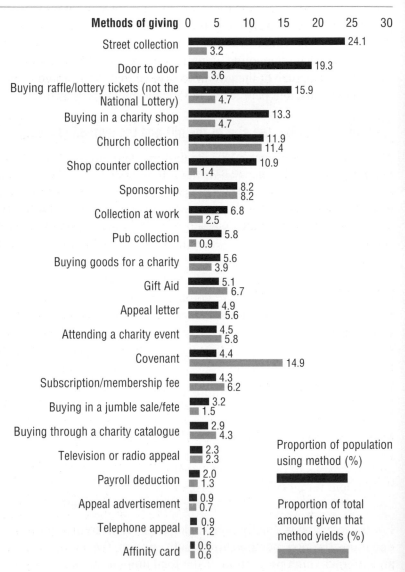

Proportion of population using method (%)

Proportion of total amount given that method yields (%)

---

[1] *Church collections are a case apart, as they attract over a tenth of the population as well as over a tenth of total donations.*

Truly large donations that run into thousands of pounds are not everyday occurrences. Therefore, the chances are that they will not be captured by a survey among the general public. Within the survey on which this section is based, various levels of donations may still be distinguished. About one-fifth of donors give on average less than £2 per month, whereas nearly a quarter give more than £20 per month. As has been shown above, there are 'small change' methods and there are methods that yield slightly larger amounts. Are these methods mutually exclusive? Do people who give more than average use only certain methods, at the expense of the humble rattling tin?

The answer is slightly more complex. Although donations of under £2 are mainly made up of door-to-door and street collections, donors giving more than £20 in total give more-than-average amounts by all methods. However, they do favour certain methods for their giving: sponsorship, church collection, responding to an appeal letter, buying in a charity shop or from a catalogue, attending an event, taking out a subscription or a covenant, and use of Gift Aid. The popular covenant ceased to be tax-effective in April 2000, and charities need to ensure conversion to Gift Aid.

Use of methods by gender

On average, more women give than men, and women give more than men. The data do not reveal why this may be, but it is constructive to see how the different ways of giving contribute to this picture. If all methods follow the overall pattern (ie men give less and less often), then it may simply be that men are less generous than women. However, if there are certain methods by which men give more, or which more of them use to give, then it may be that men and women respond differently to different fundraising approaches.

It appears that there are a few methods of giving that are very clearly male dominated: collections in the pub and at work, and through covenant and payroll. The first two of these can be explained by opportunity: those who are more likely to be in the pub or at work will also be more likely to be targeted by collections. By a similar token, it will come as little surprise that women are more frequent buyers in charity shops than men. The higher involvement of men in payroll giving probably reflects higher levels of male labour in the manufacturing industries, where the scheme tends to have been promoted more. The gender difference in giving through covenant is more perplexing. It would seem fair to assume that setting up a covenant may be more of a household decision than an individual choice. This may reflect the fact that covenants are used by an older generation, particularly by churchgoers, in traditional male-dominated households.

There are other methods that seem to vary in popularity between men and women. For example, women are more likely than men to attend a charity event or take out a subscription or membership, but men tend to spend more money through these methods. The same is true for sponsorships: more women are involved in sponsorships, but men who sponsor on average donate more.

Use of methods by age

Different age groups vary in their participation rate in different methods more than in the amounts given through them. Although most methods follow the overall patterns as described above, there are some distinct differences. As might be expected, participation in church collections increases with age. Sponsorship seems to be a relatively new method, which is not much used by people older than 55. People between 16 and 44 are most involved in collections at work and on shop counters. Whereas the youngest age group of 16–24 does not readily take part in buying from a catalogue, taking out a subscription or membership, covenants and payroll giving, they beat all other age groups when it comes to pub collections, both in participation rates and average donations.

Use of methods by social class

Buying raffle tickets, purchasing in a jumble sale or charity shop, giving in a pub and shop collections are enjoyed at similar rates by all groups. The most differentiated category is the former covenanting, which is primarily engaged in by people from social class AB.

Implications for fundraising

This section has examined how different methods of giving appeal to different types of donor. Although the current patterns seem fairly set, there are some suggestions to be made as to how existing methods of giving can be used to reach wider audiences or increase the revenue to ensure continuation of charitable giving in the future.

Methods that attract 'small change' donations may not be the most important in financial terms, but they certainly serve a purpose in drawing in people and democratising giving. These collections seem to represent the familiar face of charitable fundraising, open to people who may not otherwise get involved and ideal for those who have only small amounts to give. Methods that require any type of paperwork, even if it is writing out a cheque, may be off-putting, especially when small sums are involved. These relatively high-profile methods of small-change fundraising will, however, remain an important source of advertising, as well as income – if administration costs can be kept reasonably low.

There also seems to be scope for cross-over between different methods, for introducing groups of people who give by certain methods to alternative ways of giving. Why should women not be drawn to payroll giving, or people over 55 not be persuaded to sponsor? Maybe the more options people are presented with, the more they will be able to choose the method that suits them best on that particular occasion, even if it is not the one they would initially have thought of?

BOXED IN? STRATEGIES FOR FUNDRAISING FROM INDIVIDUALS   Joe Saxton

Strategies for net income from individual fundraising

It would be easy for the average fundraiser to become thoroughly depressed these days. Available research has meant that the charity news is peppered with stories about declining individual giving and declining trust. Many believe that donors are fed up with the fundraising activities of charities. Even the underlying themes from market research are not encouraging. When the public is asked which causes it cares about, some of Britain's biggest charities and best-known causes are left out in the cold, with disabled and homeless people, emergency and disaster relief, and the environment all mentioned by 6 per cent or less.[2]

[2] *Future Foundation's Charity Awareness Monitor, January 2001.*

However, the doom and gloom merchants on public trust, individual giving and unhappy donors are not giving the full picture. The growth in income from fundraising from individuals over the last decade has been strong in those charities that have invested in individual fundraising and continued to innovate. Indeed, many fundraisers believe that there is no such thing as donor fatigue, just marketing fatigue. The limits to fundraising growth are not in the willingness of individuals to give, but in the imagination and energy of fundraisers to innovate. This is not to say that individual donors are not treated badly on occasions, and do not get fed up with their treatment, but that this does not represent a barrier to growth in giving overall. If you ask donors what they think about telephone fundraising, for example, they will always tell you they do not like it, but it remains a highly effective fundraising tool.

The purpose of this section is to look at where growth in fundraising has come from over the last decade and make predictions for where it will come from in the next decade. Figure 4.2 sets out a framework through which an individual charity can plot its strategies for increasing net fundraising income from supporters. The same framework can be used to look at the way that the sector as a whole can increase individual giving.

There are six broad strategies set out in Figure 4.2. The first two strategies, motivation-income and motivation-cost reduction (Boxes 1 and 2), centre around the motivations of the individual donor, either to give more, or to reduce costs to the organisation. Disasters overseas or events like TV telethons are examples of situations in which people's motivation to give can be increased most successfully. The Giving Campaign aims to increase the motivations at a generic level. Individual organisations will often reposition themselves or rebrand to try and increase their appeal to donors (among other benefits).

The weakness of the motivation-income strategy is two-fold. First, the increased motivations are often governed by external events. Disasters cannot be turned on and off at the will of a fundraising strategy, and TV telethons are limited to two or three a year. Secondly, the motivation is often only short-lived. During the 'green' boom of the late 1980s, environmental organisations recruited tens of

Figure 4.2   Generic strategies for increasing net income

	Increase income	Cut costs
Supporter motivations	**Box 1** • Disasters and emergencies • Generic giving campaigns • TV telethons • Tax-effectiveness	**Box 2** • Direct debits • Self-selection on mailing frequency
Products	**Box 3** • National fundraising event • Committed giving schemes • Membership	**Box 4** • Committed giving schemes • Membership
Techniques	**Box 5** • Telephone fundraising • Street fundraising • Better regulation of raffles • Monthly standing orders	**Box 6** • Better VAT regime on direct marketing • Better regulation of raffles • Direct debits (paperless)

thousands of new supporters. As the green tide receded, only the best fundraising teams managed to convert sufficient people to committed giving to maintain their income.

The motivation-cost reduction strategy has been used only sporadically over the last decade. A number of membership organisations have successfully motivated supporters to switch from cash membership to direct debit membership by emphasising the savings to the organisation. Some charities with regular magazines have allowed supporters to request fewer magazines and emphasised the cost savings involved, but this has been all too rare.

Over the coming decade, we are likely to see an increasing number of organisations working on their branding, but it will be difficult to quantify the effect of this on fundraising income. The extensions to Gift Aid in 2000 (see Chapter 5) have created a raft of possibilities for more tax-effective giving. However, it is not yet clear whether these changes will simply motivate donors to make their existing contributions more tax-effective, or actually increase the amount people give as well.

Fundraising products to increase income and to reduce costs

The second set of strategies (Boxes 3 and 4 of Figure 4.2) is based around the development of products to increase income (the product-income strategy) and cut costs (the product-cost reduction strategy). There have been examples of the product-income strategy in a range of national fundraising events and branded committed giving schemes.[3] MacMillan Cancer Relief has developed its 'World's largest coffee morning' year on year over the last decade. This event now raises several million pounds every year and is part of the 'calendar' in many workplaces and schools. The growth in income is not because cancer care has been made more motivating, but because the framework for giving has been made easier, with an appealing brand and easy involvement. The same is true for the development of committed giving schemes and membership. The National Trust developed their centenary membership, which for the first time gives members a chance to give more than the standard membership fee on a regular basis. Child sponsorship has continued to be a successful product for a number of overseas charities. RSPCA, Friends of the Earth, Christian Aid, PDSA and the Woodland Trust are just a few of the organisations that have created and marketed branded committed giving products with considerable fundraising success. Although the fundraising bandwagon has to some extent moved on, the product-income strategy remains very powerful for organisations that wish to attract loyal, high-value supporters.

The product-cost reduction strategy is the complement to the product-income strategy. While the latter increases the income raised from each supporter, the former reduces the costs of supporter retention. It is much cheaper to retain a supporter or member on a direct debit.

---

[3] *This is a fundraising scheme that asks people for regular donations through standing orders or direct debits and creates a specific name for the scheme. Examples include Living Planet Initiative (from Friends of the Earth), Project Partners (from Oxfam), Centenary Membership (from National Trust) or the Best Friends scheme (from PDSA).*

There is no need for expensive mailings in order to generate income (although mailings may still be needed for recruitment drives). The retention rate is much higher for individuals on a direct debit or standing order, reducing the expense of recruiting new supporters simply to maintain a static database size. The same shift is true for members who move from cash or cheque subscriptions to a direct debit. Each conversion may save the cost of several renewal mailings.

The four strategies discussed so far have all been significant over the last decade (and the potential for product development over the next decade is discussed below). However, it is without doubt the next two strategies that have been most significant over the last ten years: the technique-income strategy and the technique-cost reduction strategy (Boxes 5 and 6 in Figure 4.2). These two strategies are effective for the individual organisation and for the sector as a whole.

New fundraising techniques to increase income and reduce costs

Direct response television (DRTV), telephone fundraising and street fundraising through face-to-face approaches have revolutionised recruitment of new supporters and subsequent communications. Telephone fundraising, in particular, has had a massive impact on charities' ability to convert supporters to direct debits or bankers' orders. As a technique, telephone fundraising has been used to recruit volunteers and house-to-house collectors, sign up people cold to a commitment, convert members from cash subscribers to direct debit, and even to discuss legacies.

DRTV is now a successful supporter recruitment technique for a range of charities: most emphatically for children, animal and overseas charities and with more limited success among organisations for disabled people and environmental issues. Street fundraising is probably the most successful new fundraising technique developed in the last five years, and the range of organisations that have found it successful is very diverse.

If the technique-income strategy is effective for individual charities, it has also considerable potential for the sector as a whole. The change in Gift Aid regulations has resulted in a raft of new income for charities as they convert existing donors to a tax-effective status. The development of payroll giving has given rise to a whole new way of giving which, while slow to catch on, generated £55 million in 2000/01 for charities. There is also considerable potential for the technique-income strategy in the future. The regulations for raffles/lotteries are extraordinarily restrictive and well overdue for a radical overhaul. What other area of fundraising is there where regulation limits the amount of money a charity can raise, or dictates how much fundraisers can ask for?

The power of the giving habit

It is not just the technique-income strategy that has been very powerful over the last decade; the technique-cost reduction strategy has been the other strategic driver of net income growth. The growth in direct debits over standing orders has generated savings for charities, as has the development of better print buying. The growth of out-sourced print and design work has saved some charities up to 20 per cent over their existing purchasing mechanisms, particularly if they had previously bought through one of the large direct-marketing agencies. The technique-cost reduction strategy has plenty of strategic potential left to exploit.

The task for individual charities and for the sector as a whole is to work out where the sources of net income are going to be over the next decade. Figure 4.2 can be used as a strategic tool to help identify the potential for growth. Each charity can try to identify where it is weak and strong in each of the six strategies and which of the strategies it can most effectively use to build net income. The sector as a whole can do the same and assess where energy and resources can be most successfully invested. Many are tempted to try to change people's motivations for giving, a topic more fully discussed in Chapters 7 and 8: the alternative, possibly more effective, approach lies in better fundraising techniques and better fundraising products. For example, Figure 4.3 looks at the generic potential in the area of product and technique development.

The 'giving box' in Figure 4.3 has four squares, which divide fundraising activities into 'giving', 'living', 'reactive' and 'habitual'. 'Giving' is where people are knowingly and consciously giving (raffles, donations, standing orders and collection envelopes, for

Figure 4.3 The giving box

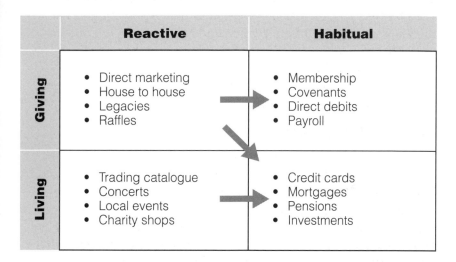

example). 'Living' is where people are carrying out some other function, but happen to be giving as they do so (buying Christmas cards, going to a concert or buying from a charity shop, for example). 'Reactive' is where people have to be asked to give; 'habitual' is where people make an initial decision but where, after that, the donations are made without further consent or requests.

The combination of these two product strands is shown in the four boxes in Figure 4.3. Put in this way, it is relatively easy to see that most of the traditional giving activities have fallen into the category of 'reactive giving' and 'reactive living'. The last decade has seen a dramatic shift from 'reactive giving' with the development of 'habitual giving'.

The greatest untapped potential may lie in the 'habitual living' category where people are giving, month in, month out, just by going about their everyday activities. Affinity credit cards have already proved that they have a role, but the market for the other affinity products is still only in its infancy. Imagine a mortgage that gave to charity every month an agreed sum on top of the interest repayments. Imagine a life insurance product that paid out an agreed percentage of the fund on maturity, or death, to a chosen charity. Imagine a pension fund that made a monthly donation direct into a tax-effective charity account. The potential is enormous, constrained only by the need to abide by the Financial Services Act.

The successes in individual giving over the last decade have come from better fundraising products and techniques and over the next decade they will come from the same strategic direction. There is no such thing as donor fatigue, only marketing fatigue.

THE POTENTIAL OF THE INTERNET FOR FUTURE CHARITABLE GIVING   Howard Lake

'The internet will be the single most important driver of change in charities over the next decade' (Saxton and Game, 2001). This was the conclusion of *Virtual Promise*, the most recent research on how British charities are making use of the internet. The report found that the charity sector was far from making the most of 'the internet revolution'. Despite this, the revolution in online fundraising and online giving is already well underway.

Within a month of the publication of *Virtual Promise*, it took Comic Relief just six hours to receive £1.75 million in online donations. This represented about 8 per cent of income generated on the night of the telethon. Furthermore, the ComicRelief.com website encouraged other methods of giving, including calling a telephone hotline and posting a cheque, so it will have been responsible for further income. The charity used the Web effectively, but so too did its various supporters and volunteer fundraisers. Online activities in aid of Comic Relief included online betting on hamster races, sales by Amazon.co.uk of special *Harry Potter* books, online auctions at QXL.com and blackadderhall.co.uk, and sales of merchandise from Sainsbury's online grocery site. Schools were encouraged to create their own Comic Relief Web sites, and thousands of online organisations showed their support by 'turning the web red'.

This extensive and creative embrace of the internet as a fundraising and giving medium by a household-name charity and many of its supporters indicates that the internet has become a key element in the fundraising mix. Comic Relief's online success demonstrates that the internet can prove an essential channel in charity fundraising. Very few other charities are likely to be able to emulate the scale of this success, but donors to many other charities will have experienced this online fundraising via Comic Relief. Some charities might not be fundraising directly from their supporters over the internet, but they should realise that other charities, to which their donors also donate, are doing so.

Indeed, the range of methods of fundraising and giving online has expanded considerably in the past two years. Most charities have focused narrowly on whether to accept credit card donations online. Yet the Web offers many other methods of communicating with donors and giving them an opportunity to support charities.

Fundraising events can be promoted online, and the fundraising auction in particular has been transferred online by many charities, with varying degrees of success. Oxfam GB raised £160,000 in May 2000 with a week-long auction of rock star Pete Townshend's guitars, and Breast Cancer Care raised £101,000 by auctioning Baroness Thatcher's handbag a few months later. Various online auction companies have spotted the value of attracting charities' members and supporters by offering their services free of charge to host online charity auctions. QXL.com, for example, advertises the fact that it helped British charities raise £350,556 during 2000.

Affiliate or referral marketing has been attempted by charities, although most seem to have preferred the ready-made online shopping malls offered by organisations such as free2give.co.uk, savivo.co.uk, go-help.co.uk, and itsgoodtogive.co.uk. These organisations list up to 170 online retailers selling everything from books to holidays and clothing. They negotiate a referral fee from retailers for directing paying customers to their sites, and then split their income or profits with participating charities. Charities take part by encouraging their supporters to shop online at a particular online shopping mall.

Amazon.com was one of the pioneers of online affiliate marketing in 1997. They pass on between 5 and 15 per cent of the retail price of books sold to the affiliate from whose site the purchaser visited. Charity supporters can now, if they wish, ensure that their favourite charity will earn income every time they buy a book online, provided they visit via the charity's site.

A variant on the affiliate marketing model – although it has since all but disappeared – was the free charity Internet Service Provider (ISP).[4] Supporters were able to get online with ISPs that donated a percentage of their income to one or more charities. The model was similar to the charity affinity credit card. Christian Aid pioneered this model with Surfaid in September 1997 and earned one pound a month from each subscriber.

With the introduction of subscription-free ISPs such as Freeserve the model changed a little. ISPs passed on a percentage of the call-connect charge to one or more charities, which meant that charities typically received a small percentage of the penny or so per minute it cost their supporters to go online. Waitrose.com, care4free.net, and itsgoodtogive.co.uk and many others offered this method of ongoing income generation for various charities. Oxfam is one of the few charities that offer ISP services themselves to their supporters in a deal with Yahoo!

This sense of easy or invisible giving has proved popular. The Hungersite.com has demonstrated how effective the click-to-give-for-free idea can be. Supporters click once a day at the site and view a corporate donor's advertisement. In return for this, the corporate donor makes a small donation to the charity. The Hungersite.com generated 9,502 tonnes of food aid in 2000, having generated 3,004 tonnes in the last seven months of 1999. The model has been emulated by hundreds of other charities, with the result that you can now click for cancer, the rainforest, landmines, mastectomies, children, birds and many other causes. In February 2001 WaterAid launched a successful click-to-give-for-free site with corporate sponsor Thames Water. It reached its target within two weeks instead of its anticipated three months, raising £100,000.

---

[4] *The decline of the ISP model carries its own message for charities: online fundraising models will come and go, and some of them will be short-lived, possibly working well for just a year or two. Charities that hold back from using the internet, concerned at its volatility, or that stick to long-term decision processes will be unable to benefit from the windows of opportunity it offers. Income from the ISP model was not huge, but Waitrose.com, for example, raised £20,000 in its first year, which was split between the British Red Cross, British Heart Foundation, Macmillan Cancer Relief, and the Prince's Trust.*

While credit card donations have dominated charities' thinking in terms of accepting online donations, there are other options. Sightsavers International and Comic Relief are charities that encourage donors to request a telephone call via their websites. The donor fills in an online form with their telephone contact details and a charity representative then telephones them at the charity's expense to handle their transaction or query. This live, human contact option has been available since 1997, but very few charities have offered it to their donors.[5]

Web billing is another method of online transaction that does not require a credit card. This allows donors to donate or purchase online an item such as a report and have the amount added to their telephone bill. To make the donation, donors are connected seamlessly and with their consent to a premium rate telephone line for a set time or a set fee. The companies offering this service then remit the donation back to the charity. Comic Relief used such a service for the online voting component of its Celebrity Big Brother campaign in March 2001.

E-mail payment is another under-used option for online donations. Although systems such as Paypal.com are used extensively in the USA, they have not yet been embraced in the UK, at least by charities. Systems such as the recently launched NOCHEX, supported by NatWest Bank, allow users to send payments via e-mail without the need for a credit card. Transactions are credited and debited directly to bank accounts.

CAF has offered its own alternative to online giving by credit card. Since May 1998 CAFcard holders have been able to donate securely online to any registered charity of their choice.

The changes to tax-efficient giving introduced by the government in April 2000 have yielded yet more methods of giving online. Regular payments by direct debit can now be made online, whereas previously

---

[5] *In 1996, the US Red Cross found that 35 per cent of people giving by its telephone credit-card hotline had found the number on their website. In other words, people used the website but preferred to talk to a human to transact the donation. If the charity offers to call the donor back at no charge to the donor, that should be attractive to many donors. If this is applicable across the sector, how much money have charities failed to raise over the last four or five years?*

direct debits required a written signature. Greenpeace UK was one of the first organisations to trial this system.

In addition, now that almost all donations can be made tax-efficiently under the extended Gift Aid provisions, it is possible to accept Gift Aid donations online. Although tax could be reclaimed manually on any credit card donation made with a suitable Gift Aid statement by the donor, new services are offering to handle the tax-efficient element online and effectively instantaneously. Justgiving.com is one new organisation that is offering charities such new services. It is offering the facility to accept credit card donations online and plans to collect the tax reclaim on such donations in real time.

The range of methods of giving online continues to grow, and few if any charities are taking the opportunity to test them all. The next few years will certainly see some of the dot.com fundraising companies fail or merge, and new opportunities will appear such as online lotteries and integration with interactive TV. With support from government initiatives such as UK Online and from voluntary sector umbrella bodies, together with innovation from charities and social businesses, charity supporters should continue to find an attractive, simple, low-cost and appropriate method of giving online.

WHERE NOW FOR LEGACY FUNDRAISING? Richard Radcliffe

Legacies are a special case – they have become the least tax-effective way of giving to charity. Why is this? The average legator (legacy donor) dies with an estate value well under the tax threshold, and those who leave residuary legacies tend to be less wealthy than those who give cash legacies. So, inheritance tax savings are not really a carrot. Legacies cannot be paid under a Gift Aid payment because they are gifts from capital rather than income.

On the other hand, it is not clear that it would make any difference if the Chancellor decided to include tax benefits for estates of all values. Focus group research has repeatedly made it clear that the lowest motivator for leaving a charitable legacy is 'tax-effectiveness'. The exception is wealthy people, who often set up a trust and distribute income rather than capital. This is what Christina Foyle did when she left the largest-ever legacy for charitable purposes (£59 million) in 1999.

Watershed demographics

Legacy giving is at a watershed, which might turn into a flood or a small puddle. Extending the water analogy, the legacy sea over the next half century holds tidal waves of threats and opportunities that need addressing now.

We are entering a period of real change. The British annual death rate, at around 1 per cent of the population, has been relatively static for well over 100 years. But the annual *number* of deaths, due to the first baby boomer period, is going to increase over the next 40 years by 25 per cent or more. The number of people aged 65+ will almost double, so there are many more 'legacy targets'.

Against this tide of excitement there will be a strong undertow (for charities and families). We are all living longer and more of us will need residential care. Assets will be used up and elderly people will, understandably, worry about 'what will be left over'. So, residuary legacies (current average value to charity around £23,000; cash legacies are around £3,000) are at risk because there might be nothing, or little, left over. This threatening asset eroder is already making elderly people sit up and say 'Let's wait and see about including a charitable legacy' – and, not surprisingly, many will wait until it is too late.

We are also living in an era of rapidly changing lifestyles. Most elderly people, still, have traditional values: they regularly attend places of worship, they like to have the family sitting round a table for Sunday lunch and they like to save money. Many of their children are 'Thatcher babes' and do not need an inheritance; their grandchildren may not share their values at all. As a result, feeling antipathy to their apparently consumerist life-styles, granny (68 per cent of legators are female) may leave everything to a favourite animal charity.

There is also the power of the 'single household' charging through the next generation, the person who is childless, widowed, divorced, or single by choice. Divorcees might have more than one family and have little to spare at death time. But the others will be liquid rich and asset rich – their mail boxes over the next 40 years will be attractive targets.

Finally, we have an increasingly multi-ethnic, multicultural society. First-generation immigrants tend to leave any legacies to their original homeland; second-generation immigrants are more likely to be looking internally within Britain, so there is possibly a large change in terms of causal support areas. The increasingly non-religious nature of society may also cause problems. Many practising Jews and Christians are tithers who give 10 per cent of their income to charity and then 10 per cent of their estate to their church/synagogue or Jewish/Christian causes. Will tithing survive into the future?

Today's discriminatory donor

Nowadays social conscience and social awareness are much more widespread and critical. So can you really rely on people reading the odd advertisement and thinking 'Yes, I will leave £23,000 to that charity'?

No. The donor of the 'dead giveaway' will be a thinking donor who has been through, or been affected by, an experience that has marked their life, such as cancer, disability, religious conversion. They will want to make a real difference and they will want a legacy to be *their* choice. The days of the discriminatory donor have arrived.

There is another unknown factor. Many donors in their 40s and 50s (the second baby boom) were brought up in the era of campaigning rather than pure charitable work; Greenpeace and its Rainbow Warrior are probably the best examples from the early 1970s. When these supporters grow old, will they want to keep campaigning organisations in their will or will they have tired of campaigning? If they suffer experiences of ill health or, more positively, visit nice stately homes with their grandchildren, will they turn into traditional givers and revert to 'giving to charity'?

There is concern that insensitive fundraising is leading people to take legacies out of wills: there have been a number of reports of charities that have been regular beneficiaries of legacy income in the past, but from which prospective legators have recently been withdrawing their support. We do not know whether this is something that used to happen in the past, but instinct suggests it is something that is on the increase.

Legators provide around £1.5 billion a year to charities, and the average gift value is an astonishing £13,000. But the donor pool is shrinking, and income could turn into a puddle if we continue to fail to meet donors' attitudes, motivations and expectations.

All these external influences surrounding the legacy marketplace make it very difficult to forecast the future. No economic forecasting model can help us, because many of the influences are attitudinal rather than economic. This is bad news for trustees, who will have to make an educated guess as to what their future legacy income will be. On the other hand, however, only 5 per cent of those who die leave a legacy to charity, compared with 80 per cent of people who give to charity in their lifetime. So the marketplace has great growth potential.

The past and the present

Old-time legacy fundraising focused on informing solicitors on the need to promote legacies to their clients. But how many people would obey their solicitor's recommendations? Would they rather follow their heart?

Legacy fundraising strategies for large charities are moving fast in terms of the words and pictures used. It is to be hoped that these moves are in the right direction to have a real impact in the sector, because the growth rate in the marketplace has been almost static for the last 10 years. So what is happening?

Recognising that all fundraising is sensitive, but legacy fundraising exceptionally so, let us make it personal for a moment. Take my 84-year-old mother – she is a typical target. She has had a stroke but is her usual cheerful philanthropic self. She supports many charities – some in a planned way and others spontaneously. How would I like her to be approached for a legacy? And how would she like to be approached? The answers are simple:

- I would not want her to be asked, because I will inherit less.
- She would not answer a letter asking for a legacy, but might send £10–£20 instead.
- She would not read a newsletter from cover to cover and would forget most messages before she next consults her solicitor.

AN OVERVIEW OF TAX-EFFECTIVE GIVING
Cathy Pharoah and Catherine Walker

Tax-effective giving – the schemes and reliefs available

'Tax-effective giving' is often used rather loosely in Britain as if it were a brand in itself, but it actually refers to a restricted range of ways of giving money that attract tax reliefs. These are broadly:

- making gifts through the Gift Aid scheme;
- making gifts of assets, including shares and securities;
- payroll giving – giving directly from pay before it is taxed;
- giving by covenants (now being phased out as tax-effective vehicles for giving);
- bequeathing legacies, or parts of legacies, to charity.

In rare instances, British charitable tax reliefs can add as much as 80 per cent to the value of a gift; in others, they can be used to reduce the 'cost' or 'price' of a gift by this amount. A gift of £1,000 in shares may cost the donor only £200, because he or she receives £400 of higher-rate income tax relief on the gift, and up to £400 of capital gains tax relief. This is only a bargain, of course, if the donor wants to make a gift in the first place.

Although the range of tax reliefs on giving available in the UK is quite restricted and much less complex than in the USA, it is often seen as complicated because these different ways of making 'tax-effective' gifts have been in existence for different lengths of time and are subject to different rules. The recent changes to the system for acquiring tax reliefs on giving, introduced by the government in the 2000 Budget, were partly aimed at simplifying and unifying these procedures to make tax-effective giving generally more accessible.

Types of tax-effective giving

Gift Aid is a system whereby an individual can give a one-off donation to charity, and the charity can reclaim the basic-rate income tax (22 per cent in the 2001/2002 tax year) on it (or a company can make gross payments and get a corporation tax deduction). At the higher income tax bracket, the charity gets 22 per cent tax relief, and the donor gets the other 18 per cent. Minimum limits to gifts ceased to be in force as from April 2000, and all gifts, including small one-off gifts, may now be tax-effective as long as the donor declares tax status. The paperwork for both parties was simplified, and donors can now use Gift Aid by phone or internet, removing the previous need to sign a form.[1]

Payroll giving is currently available to employees on PAYE if their employers offer a scheme. Donations are made direct from salary, before tax, and the tax relief is given to the donor, thus reducing the cost of the gift/donation. As from April 2000 the maximum limit was abolished, allowing much larger gifts from the payroll. In addition to this, a supplement of 10 per cent on all donations will be paid to charities by the government for a period of three years.

Income tax relief on gifts of shares and securities As from April 2000, a new income tax relief came into effect on gifts to charities of shares and securities of listed companies, at their current market value. Where higher-rate tax of 40 per cent is payable, full tax relief at this rate is allowed. Gifts of shares and securities also receive capital gains tax relief. It also became easier for those who wish to make charitable gifts out of the interest from trusts to obtain income tax relief on the charitable element of the income.

Deeds of covenant have been the most popular form of tax-effective giving. They are legally enforceable commitments to pay a fixed amount regularly to charity over a period of more than three years.

As from April 2000, covenants ceased to be tax-effective forms of giving; existing covenants will, however, be honoured until they have run their full term, and charities may now make covenanted gifts tax-effective through Gift Aid.

Legacies Gifts and bequests to charities are generally exempt from the 40 per cent inheritance tax (and there is no capital gains tax on death).

---

[1] *Millennium Gift Aid was introduced by the government in 1998 as a special case of Gift Aid. The minimum gift was £100 (payable in instalments if the donor desired), and all donations went only to charities dedicated to helping the world's poorest countries, and refugees from Kosovo. Millennium Gift Aid officially ended on 31 December 2000.*

Capital gains tax (CGT) relief on gifts of assets Gifts to charities qualify for no gain/no loss relief from capital gains tax (CGT).

The IR website (http://www.inlandrevenue.gov.uk) is a good source of reference for further detail on the rules relating to charitable tax reliefs. Chapter 3 provides details of the amount of money raised by the different tax-effective giving mechanisms. Unfortunately, the IR is unable to provide estimates for the value of CGT reliefs on gifts to charities.

Who gives tax-effectively?

Tax-effective giving in Britain has been taken up by about 5 per cent of the population, although by 11 per cent of givers. Use of the schemes before the tax changes (in 2001) was split between the main tax-effective giving schemes as follows (CAF/IR/NCVO 1999):[2]

- 3 per cent of the population used covenants.
- 2 per cent of the population participated in payroll deduction schemes.
- Less than 1 per cent of the population gave through Gift Aid (and only 0.2 per cent through Millennium Gift Aid).

Tax-effective givers traditionally differ from non-tax-effective givers in a similar (but exaggerated) way to the way donors differ from non-donors. Tax-effective givers are from a higher social class, and are more likely to be married, to be the male head of the household, to have been educated further, in a full-time job, earning more money and giving significantly more per month than non tax-effective givers. Based on survey data from July 2000, tax-effective givers were donating on average £61.42 in a month compared with £8.21 on average donated by non-tax-effective givers (CAF/IR/NCVO 2000).

Evidence from the same survey additionally suggests some differences in attitudes towards giving, with tax-effective givers being significantly more likely to consider important the kind of cause and the trustworthiness of the charity in their decision to donate. They are also more likely to feel that their donations matter to the charity and that they have a duty to give and not to rely on others to give. This

---

[2]   *These figures are likely to underestimate levels of bigger gifts, which are thinly spread throughout the population – see Chapter 3.*

suggests that tax-effective givers may be more committed and involved in their giving than others.

Who uses which scheme?

There are some small but significant differences in age between people using different tax-effective schemes. Covenants have generally been preferred by older, higher-income individuals. Payroll givers are spread across all age bands, with a majority in the 35–44 group. Gift Aid use has been confined to those over 35 years of age. Interestingly, Millennium Gift Aid was largely taken up by its target audience – young people, the lowest paid and elderly people – although overall uptake was very low.

While the greatest benefit of charitable tax reliefs is to charities, there are also fiscal inducements for the donor, as has been discussed. Of course, the value of a tax relief to the individual is directly related to how much tax the individual pays, and schemes that offer tax savings are therefore often more attractive to the wealthier section of the community, which, in absolute terms, pays more tax. Not surprisingly, the evidence available shows how rich people make much more use of tax-effective giving than the less well-off (see Table 5.1).

Table 5.1 Relationship between average income and use of tax-effective giving

Average annual household income (£)	Uses payroll giving (%)	Uses covenants (%)	Uses Gift Aid (%)
2,500–7,500	0.0	0.5	0.0
7,500–<13,500	0.0	4.7	2.0
13,500–<25,000	2.4	5.3	0.0
25,000–<35,000	5.7	6.9	1.0
>35,000	8.8	6.6	4.0
Higher earners[1]	10.0	47.0	7.0

Source CAF/IR/NCVO (1999).

[1]The figures in this line are derived from an unpublished survey of a number of higher-rate taxpayers by CAF/IR in 1999, and reflect the high level of giving through covenants among this group (although this was not a representative sample).

Wealthier people are also more aware of the actual and potential value of tax reliefs on giving. Table 5.2 illustrates the difference in interest in charitable tax reliefs among the different social groups. People in the AB social group are two and a half times more likely to see themselves as using tax-effective methods of giving in the future than those in the DE social group.

Major donors

In introducing new charitable tax reliefs to stimulate giving, government policy was designed to be equitable. On the one hand, it encouraged more and bigger gifts from wealthy donors; on the other, it was concerned that any extension of the schemes should make benefits more available to less well-off donors and those making smaller gifts.

The main change likely to persuade the wealthy to give more was the introduction of income tax relief on the current market value of shares and securities. Almost one-fifth of the population now owns shares and securities, and their value is over £250 billion. Demutualisation shares worth £5 billion were sold by the public in 1998, showing the potential of shares as a source of income to charities. Figures from CAF's client population of tax-effective givers show that only about 2 per cent give shares and securities, although the number increased by a half after the new income tax benefit was introduced.

Table 5.2 Relationship between social group and interest in tax reliefs

Social class	Likely to use tax-effective methods in future (%)
AB	44
C1	38
C2	18
DE	17

Source CAF/IR/NCVO (1999).

Democratising access to charitable tax reliefs

The two planks of policy to make tax-effective giving more accessible were to make Gift Aid relief available on all sizes of gift, and to encourage use of payroll giving, which brings full tax relief at source on donations of every size and is accessible to every type of worker through the payroll. Each of these initiatives will now be reviewed in turn.

Gift Aid comes of age

As Figure 5.1 shows, the amount given using the Gift Aid scheme grew steadily over the ten-year period following its introduction, from 1990 to 2000. The upper limit for gifts was abolished in 1991, and the minimum limit was lowered to £250 in 1993. These revisions did not alter growth trends. Individual donations over the ten years totalled just over £2 billion, with company gifts adding a very similar figure, bringing the total raised through the Gift Aid scheme in the last decade to just over £4 billion. In its decade of existence, Gift Aid has been the fastest growing tax-effective scheme in Britain, increasing from just 9,390 donations in 1990/1991 to over 300,000 donations in 1999/2000. This growth undoubtedly influenced the government's decision to widen access to Gift Aid.

Long-term trends and recent growth in Gift Aid donations

The figures show almost continuous growth in individuals' giving through Gift Aid, except for a one-off drop in 1995/96. The reasons for that drop are not obvious; nor is it clear why there were quite dramatic increases after that point. It is interesting to note, however, that this increase coincided with the first general increase in total public donations for five years (NCVO/NOP 1998), also noticeable in the FES figures published by CAF.

One possible explanation for these increases may be the economic and psychological changes in Britain following the general election in 1997. Some commentators have suggested a 'demonstration effect' of government policy on people's giving (Jones et al, 1998). In other words, the new Labour government may have encouraged more giving by placing a noticeable emphasis on public-sector welfare spending, on the expansion of the voluntary sector and a 'new giving age'. Similarly, falling interest rates and the accompanying bolstering of the national economy, with declining rates of unemployment, have produced positive economic and psychological effects. Even the expectations of any of these things happening could encourage a more positive attitude towards charitable giving.

The growth potential for Gift Aid and first indications of change

From survey data gathered before the tax changes came into effect, CAF and NCVO were able to model the potential impact of these changes on individual donations, based on what people said they would do and on estimates of the incentive effect of the tax reliefs (CAF/IR/NCVO 1999). These models estimated a potential gain to the sector of £200–£400 million per annum as a result of the tax changes.

The most recent surveys have shown an increase from less than 1 per cent to 11 per cent of the adult population of Britain using Gift Aid by July 2001 (CAF/IR/NCVO 2001). If charities reclaim the tax on these donations, the potential gain in tax reliefs could be around £250 million in the first year of the new scheme, as predicted in the models.

Figure 5.1 Amount donated through Gift Aid by individuals, 1990–2000 (£ million)

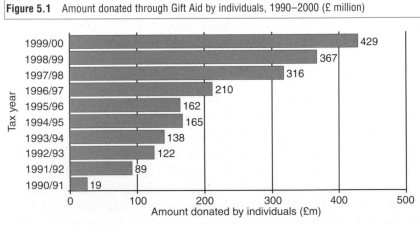

Source IR statistics, 2000.

Although the take-up of new Gift Aid has increased, however, it still represents only one-fifth of all tax-paying donors, and around one-quarter of the total amount given to charity in a month.

Yet the potential for increasing this amount is huge. Overall levels of participation and amounts given have not yet changed substantially since the tax changes, nor has the general profile of donors using new Gift Aid. This probably indicates that charities are targeting primarily those donors who have already used Gift Aid or other tax-effective methods, or those with similar profiles, who they may feel are most likely to convert.

There are, however, encouraging indications of a levelling-out of the gender balance in a previously male-dominated group, and of a movement towards tax-effective giving becoming more inclusive, opening the way towards the 'tax-effective giving for all' ideal embodied in the tax changes of the 2000 Budget.

There are also small signs that charities could benefit from looking towards other donor groups to widen the profile of tax-effective givers. The fact is that, in their first year, the tax changes in themselves appear to have attracted an extra 7 per cent of the population to give for the first time. These new givers are younger, with lower incomes and mainly from social class DE; less than one-third of them were asked to convert their gifts to new Gift Aid. This suggests that, alongside attracting conversion of gifts to Gift Aid, the publicity surrounding the tax changes may have had a secondary effect of raising the overall profile of giving in Britain.

The convertibility of different giving mechanisms

In developing fundraising strategies for the future, charities will be well aware that certain giving mechanisms are more amenable to conversion to Gift Aid than others. Figure 5.2 ranks each giving method from the most popular (street collection) to the least popular (appeal advertisement) in terms of its use by the general public. It shows how, for example, 81 per cent of donors giving by covenant, 53 per cent of direct debit and standing order users, and only 1 per cent of street collection donors converted their donation to Gift Aid (CAF/IR/NCVO 2001).

Figure 5.2 Proportion of donors converting their gifts to Gift Aid, ranked by general popularity of use of method (%)

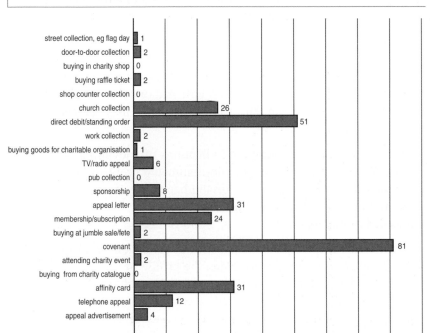

The proportion of the amount raised that was converted to Gift Aid also varies for each fundraising method. Almost all of the amount raised through covenants in March 2001 (87 per cent) was converted to Gift Aid, but only 14 per cent of the total raised through direct debits and standing orders and 7 per cent of that raised through street collections. Will charities begin to focus on the methods that yield most tax? If they do, does that mean that, rather than widening the populations of donors approached, they might narrow it?

A bright future for Gift Aid?

Since April 2000, Gift Aid has been open to all taxpayers in Britain, regardless of the size or regularity of their gift, as long as donors had paid sufficient tax. Most people (80 per cent) found it easy to convert to the new Gift Aid. Charities, with the help of the Giving Campaign, must promote awareness and understanding of the scheme, widen their target audience for tax-effective giving to all eligible gifts, allay any donor fears over divulging their tax status, and claim back the tax reliefs in a timely way.

Of course, there are costs attached to these activities for the charities – despite the simplifications there still needs to be an identifiable audit trail for the IR. This may deter some charities, especially the smaller ones, from reclaiming tax on all eligible donations, and may encourage some to concentrate, at least at first, only on donations over a certain amount. Some charities may choose to put off reclaiming tax until they have a suitable system in place, or may contract out the administration to outside service providers, such as CAF, who will do the job for them. This is discussed further below by Mark Robson.

If the challenges can be met, then Gift Aid really does have a bright and almost limitless future. But while it is a potentially highly effective way for charities to benefit from government tax breaks, the million-dollar question is whether tax breaks can also stimulate greater giving. At present, there is no data on this.

Do government tax reliefs leverage extra donations?

Government support to general charities in the form of grants and contracts is about £1 billion per annum (this excludes housing associations). If the government wants to support the work of charities, why not simply increase their grants, instead of setting up a more complicated, more unpredictable and possibly more costly system of individual tax reliefs? The arguments in favour of charitable tax reliefs over government grants are, first, the moral one that they give individuals more control over what gets supported and, second, the economic one that they have the power to leverage even more money to charities through greater individual giving.

Are charitable tax reliefs the right way to increase charitable income?

The moral argument is important both to justify the reduction in public expenditure that charitable tax reliefs entail, and also because the economic argument is weak without it. The economist's line is that, since the effect of increasing charitable tax reliefs is to 'lower' the price of giving, people will make more gifts. This only works, however, if people want to make more charitable gifts. Why should they? Both the Conservatives and New Labour have beliefs about why individuals would want to support the work of charities, and why fiscal incentives would help. Their different ideological stances were summarised by Gordon Brown:

> [During the Thatcher years] there grew a sense that individual initiative was stifled ... and that personal responsibility was undermined. [Thatcher's] view was that individuals should be left on their own, and that this was to be achieved by a withering away of the state. The thinking was summarised in what was her most famous remark: 'There is no such thing as society' ... This is a wholly different and, in my view, unacceptable view of the relationship between individual, community and government.
>
> So at the centre of my vision of society is a simple truth. Not the individual glorying in isolation ... but literally at home in society, and feeling at home because he is part not only of a family, but of a neighbourhood, a community and a social network ... This is my idea of Britain – because there is such a thing as society.
>
> To help in this, I first want to put charities on a firm foundation for the future. But I want that foundation to be the same that charities themselves want – a base of support from givers. So first, to back local initiatives by exploiting the new tax regime, we are planning to boost charitable giving by individuals.
>
> (NCVO Annual Conference, January 2000)

In other words, the particular attraction of tax relief on individual giving is that it allows individuals to express their preferences about which charities should benefit from government money and that it therefore increases personal responsibility and a sense of belonging in the community: a win–win for the individual, the charity and the community. Another view is to see charitable tax reliefs as a self-imposed limitation on government taxing power – its purpose being directly to leave to individual discretion some decisions about the allocation of resources for public purposes, where the individual is willing to forgo a portion of his or her personal resources for the same purpose (Yarmolinsky, 2000).

But while all sides seem to agree that allowing individuals greater discretion or control over spending for public benefit is a good thing, what is the effect in practice of this policy? The first point is that the absolute value of tax reliefs is highest for the wealthy (see Table 5.3), and therefore charitable tax reliefs are likely to benefit first and foremost those charities that the wealthy support. The second point is that there is clear evidence that the wealthy and the less well-off support different types of charity. In other words, charitable tax reliefs have a distortionary effect and give the preferences of the richer groups greatest weight.

As Banks and Tanner point out:

> evidence on giving patterns suggests that preferences for giving to different kinds of charities do vary across individuals in a systematic way, particularly with their income ... richer givers are more likely than poorer givers to give to charities in culture and arts, education, recreation and leisure, environment and economic, social and community development. Poorer individuals are more likely than richer ones to give to international aid charities and animal charities.

(Banks and Tanner, 1998)

Table 5.3   Differences between donors in tax status and levels of giving, by tax band

Marginal tax rate (%)	GB population[1] (%)	Average annual gift[2] (£)	Total given (£bn)
0	42	106	1.859
20/23	53	111	2.657
40	5	172	0.412
Overall	100	112	4.928

[1]IR Statistics, 1998.
[2]Passey et al (2000).

In extending tax reliefs to even the smallest gifts through the new Gift Aid scheme, the potential imbalance is being addressed, but it would take a significant increase in the numbers of small gifts to compensate for the additional tax reliefs likely to be awarded to large gifts.

Furthermore, allowing tax reliefs to follow individual preference may not automatically help those charities that find it difficult to raise money, even though they are providing for important social needs – the so-called 'unpopular' causes. Evidence from CAF's analysis of the top 500 fundraising charities shows the scale of the challenge for less-well-supported causes. For example, the public donates about £357 million each year to international agencies, and a further £336 million to cancer-related causes. By contrast, income to charities for physically disabled people was £105 million, and to mental health charities was £35 million. A policy of increasing income through tax reliefs on individual giving may not be enough by itself to help such causes. Data from the survey of the top 500 fundraising charities shows that, although voluntary support for causes such as mental, visual or hearing disability grew at a rate of around 30 per cent between 1995 and 1999, voluntary support for causes such as health grew at 95 per cent and recreation at 55 per cent.

If government opts for growth based on tax reliefs on individual giving, it is important that the public is helped to understand these issues, and that wealthy new donors are encouraged to direct funds towards needy areas and not simply to the causes or charities that their peers have been inclined to support. The extent to which people's beliefs about the role of tax and tax reliefs influence their decisions about giving is taken up further in Chapter 7. Mark Robson discusses the overall effects of fiscal policy in a later section of this chapter.

Do increases in charitable tax reliefs make us give more?

Research carried out before the recent radical changes to income tax reliefs calculated that changes to British tax reliefs have small effects on total giving and charity income. For example, one study has shown that charity income increases by 50 per cent of any additional tax relief (Jones and Posnett, 1991). In recent research, 5 per cent of tax-efficient donors said that fiscal incentives had persuaded them to give more than they would otherwise have done, while 1 per cent would not have given without the tax advantage (CAF/IR/NCVO 2000). Most gave up to 25 per cent extra on top of the value of their gift as a result of the tax advantage. The latest research using British data has shown a net positive effect of tax incentives on the volume of individual donations (Foster et al, 2000).

Although a majority of the general public in the CAF/IR/NCVO 2000 survey claimed that they had not changed the way they gave since the tax changes in April 2000, 5 per cent said they gave more money (3 per cent gave less); 4 per cent said they gave a greater number of gifts (2 per cent gave fewer), while 4 per cent said they gave to more charities (3 per cent gave to fewer). CAF, among others, is monitoring whether the new changes ultimately have a dramatic impact on charity resources. There has been significant growth in payroll giving, and in giving shares (see below).

Do increases in charitable tax reliefs make more people give?

As noted already (Banks and Tanner, 1997), the proportion of households and the proportion of people who give to charity have been in a steady decline (NCVO/NOP 1995–97). The first year since the tax changes has shown no change, but this is not a long enough time period to test their impact. About 68 per cent of people and 28 per cent of households give to charity.

Tax benefits for donors or charities?

Many in Britain have lobbied for the introduction of US-style tax reliefs, in which the full benefit always goes to the donor rather than the charity, in the belief that this would increase giving. UK research evidence does not appear to support this. Almost half of all givers (46 per cent) feel that it is *unimportant* to them to be able to give in a way whereby they could reduce their own tax bill, and only 23 per cent feel this is important or very important. However, individuals with higher incomes, in higher social classes (see Table 5.4) and of an older age are more likely to consider this important. Since such donors are responsible for many major gifts to the sector, the possible incentive effects of donor benefits should be further researched.

Table 5.4 The importance attached to tax reliefs on giving for (a) charities and (b) donors themselves, by social class

Social class	Proportion of each social class who rate tax back to the charity as important (%)	Proportion of each social class who rate tax back to the donor as unimportant (%)
AB	50	50
C1	46	45
C2	49	42
DE	39	36

Source CAF/IR/NCVO 1999.

Lack of awareness and information – diluting the effects

Although there is little evidence of any strong link between levels of tax benefits and levels of giving, it is very clear that the take-up of tax benefits is inhibited by poor knowledge. The figures in Table 5.5 show how strongly awareness of tax benefits is linked to social class.

Table 5.5 Relationship between social class and awareness of tax-effective giving

Social class	Proportion of individuals in each class who are aware of tax-effective giving (%)	
	1999	2000
AB	72	84
C1	52	62
C2	34	47
DE	27	33

Source CAF/IR/NCVO 2000.

In fact, lack of understanding of tax-effective giving mechanisms is not confined to social classes DE. Only about one-half of higher-rate tax payers can name any method of tax-effective giving when asked blind, while not all of those actually using tax-effective schemes can correctly identify whether they, or the charity, benefit from the tax relief (CAF/IR/NCVO 1999).

Raising awareness

How far can levels of tax literacy be raised? It is encouraging to find that the effect of the charities' tax changes has been to raise awareness in the general population (see Table 5.6).

Awareness has increased in all demographic groups since the tax changes were introduced, although it is still higher among higher-age, -income and -social-class groups (see Table 5.5).

Awareness, however, does not always coincide with understanding of tax-effective schemes, or use of them. Knowledge of the tax changes proves to be slightly lower (32 per cent of the population, according to CAF/IR/NCVO 2001) than general awareness of tax-effective giving. Knowledge was highest among those who were already aware of tax-effective giving schemes. The Charities Tax Review process and subsequent changes in provisions appear to have stimulated higher levels of awareness, but there is still some way to go to bring this information to the attention of the majority of the population.

Table 5.6   Increases in awareness of tax-effective giving in the general population, 2000–2001

	Proportion of population aware of tax-effective giving (%)
July 1999	43
July 2000	50
March 2001	54

Source CAF/IR/NCVO 2001.

Why more people do not use tax-effective methods of giving to charity

Besides awareness and knowledge, barriers to the take-up of tax benefits include indifference, insufficient financial means, and the difficulty of the operation (see Table 5.7). As noted earlier, results of research since the tax changes indicate that people find new Gift Aid easy to use, and this is encouraging.

The role of financial intermediaries and donor advice

The complications of tax-effective giving suggest that financial intermediaries (financial advisers, financial planners, accountants and solicitors) could play a much bigger role in providing charitable tax advice as a routine part of the financial advice they give clients.

In the USA, charitable giving advice has become the domain of a whole new profession, generally referred to as 'donor advice' and provided by 'planned giving advisors'. These are a new breed of fundraisers, knowledgeable about both donor tax benefits and also the charity universe. Their aim is generally to link tax advice with up-to-date charitable information and to help donors identify what they want to support. These ideas are beginning to catch on in the UK. The last few years have seen a plethora of new initiatives around donor advice. These include: Project Connect, which attempts to

Table 5.7   Reasons given by individuals for not using tax-efficient methods (%)

Reasons for not using tax efficient methods	Individuals (%)
Not interested	38
Don't know how to	13
Too difficult	10
Prefer to give spontaneously	7
Cannot afford it	6
Do not give enough money	3
Haven't got round to it	1
Invades my privacy	1

Source CAF/IR/NCVO 1999.

match wealthy donors with specific projects; the Association of Charitable Foundations' (ACF) promotion of new trusts through advice to individuals on setting up trusts; and the general promotion of 'venture philanthropy', the encouragement of wealthy entrepreneurs to support social enterprises, possibly through new forms of loan finance. In addition to this, the Giving Campaign has a major initiative to encourage financial advisors to provide information on charitable giving to their clients.

PAYROLL GIVING: ACCESS TO CHARITABLE TAX RELIEFS THROUGH THE PAYROLL   Debbie Romney-Alexander

Giving through the payroll today brings a method of simple, regular, tax-effective giving to all employees, whatever their salary, as long as their employer has signed up to a scheme.

Payroll giving was first introduced in Britain in the early 1900s, when Barnardo's introduced their post-tax charity payroll-giving scheme. In post-tax schemes, individual charities persuaded employers to run payroll giving, and the money was forwarded directly to the charity. These often involved very small contributions. The Barnardo's scheme was called the *National Farthing League*, with employees giving one farthing per week from their wages.

Tax benefits on gifts made through the payroll were introduced in the 1986 budget. The first pre-tax payroll-giving schemes in Britain (such as CAF's Give As You Earn) were launched in April 1987. In tax-effective payroll-giving schemes, the donation is made before tax is paid, with the resulting tax benefit going directly to the donor.

Tax-effective schemes are administered through agency charities, so that employers no longer make payments direct to individual charities. This has led to greater donor choice, with payroll givers being able to support any British registered charity through their payroll donations.

Giving through the payroll has many strengths and advantages:

• Payroll giving is easy for the donor and the employer.
• Few people leave payroll-giving schemes once they join.
• Donors can give any amount from their salary.

83

- Providing a payroll-giving scheme is good PR for companies, and research has shown that providing schemes and getting involved with good causes can increase employee loyalty.
- Charities gain from regular, committed giving through the payroll. Some companies even 'match' their employees' contributions to charity.

The potential for growth

Payroll giving has grown slowly but steadily since its introduction, with £55 million of British voluntary sector income being donated through the payroll in 2000/01.

In Britain, just 1 per cent of employers and around 3 per cent of eligible employees currently participate in payroll-giving schemes. In a co-ordinated effort to increase charitable giving through the payroll, the British government introduced tax changes in the April 2000 Budget to make payroll giving more attractive. These changes were:

- the abolition of the £100 per month upper limit on tax-effective donations through the payroll;
- an additional 10 per cent added to all payroll donations for a period of three years.

At the same time a three-year nationwide payroll-giving campaign was launched. The government hopes that these initiatives will encourage large-scale take-up of payroll giving and help to realise its huge potential. Early indications suggest that these measures are already having a big impact. In 2000–01, the year following the tax changes, payroll giving increased by £12 million, a 29 per cent growth on the previous Children's Promise Millennium Campaign (see p 88).

Profile of the payroll giver

Payroll giving attracts givers who are not generally attracted by other tax-effective giving methods. As Table 5.8 shows, payroll givers are younger, on a lower income, less well-educated, and more likely to be male than taxpayers in general (those in PAYE).

Table 5.8 Payroll givers compared with taxpayers in general (%)

	Payroll givers (%)	All those in PAYE (%)
Age 30–39 years	31	27
Male	74	55
Female	26	45
Left formal education aged 16 years	55	46

Source Family Resources Survey 1995–96 (ONS, 1996), as reported in Banks and Tanner, 1998.

Payroll giving is also better represented in the north, Yorkshire and the West Midlands, with the reverse being true in London and the south-east of England, as Table 5.9 demonstrates.

Payroll giving opened up tax-effective giving for people on all income levels and was targeted at all groups of people, including those in the manufacturing industries who may previously not have considered regular charitable giving. This probably explains to some extent the regional north–south split and the high proportion of men in payroll-giving schemes.

Table 5.9 Geographical distribution of payroll givers and taxpayers in general (%)

	Payroll givers (%)	All those in PAYE (%)
North	10	6
Yorkshire	11	9
West Midlands	14	9
London	6	10
South-east	17	22

Source Family Resources Survey 1995–96 (ONS, 1996), as reported in Banks and Tanner, 1998.

Importance to the donor of the tax incentive

The tax incentive is an important aspect of payroll giving. One of the main differences between this method and Gift Aid is that, with payroll giving, the donor can benefit from the whole tax relief. Currently, higher-rate taxpayers are exempt from paying 40 per cent tax on payroll donations, while basic-rate taxpayers are exempt from 22 per cent tax. Being able to give £10 per month to charity at a cost of only £7.80 can be a significant factor for lower givers on lower incomes.

A new approach to marketing?

In general, it is difficult to sell tax efficiency to the wider population. Payroll giving has traditionally been marketed by emphasising the value to the donor of the tax benefit. This in fact undersells the potential gain, which can be up to 83 per cent extra on payroll donations. Perhaps it is time for change.

A promotion of the benefit to the charity (as opposed to the donor) and a fresh approach to marketing could realise substantial gains in payroll-giving income to charities.[2] This may well be the sea change needed to encourage charities to use more of their resources to promote payroll giving.

The scheme does, however, have some operational disadvantages, which may be restricting its uptake by charities and employers. Three of these are discussed below.

Increasing the size of payroll donations

A CAF survey found that almost 90 per cent of payroll givers had never been asked to increase the size of their donation. The value of payroll donations is therefore gradually eroded by inflation. Whose responsibility should it be to ask payroll givers to increase the size of their donation: employers, charities or payroll-giving agencies?

---

[2] *For example, a higher-rate taxpayer who wished to give a net donation of £10 per month through the payroll would need to pledge £16.66 per month, the gross figure before tax. An extra 10 per cent would then be added to this gross figure by the government, making the donation worth £18.30, an 83 per cent increase on the original £10 donation. This is an enormous added value for the charity.*

Research has shown that many payroll givers would increase the amount they give if asked to do so. Asking payroll givers to increase the amount they give on an annual basis, for example by leaving a form on their desk, may encourage an increase in the size of gifts. Most British charities, agency charities and professional fundraising organisations (PFOs) concentrate on payroll-giving recruitment, not increasing the donations of current subscribers.

The increasing trend of using PFOs to recruit payroll givers has probably been responsible, in part, for the growth in employee participation and payroll-giving income in Britain in recent years. However, the tendency for PFOs to ask for smaller monthly contributions (for example, £5) could either be responsible for bringing greater numbers of people into schemes, or for restricting the amount these same people would give. If asked to give more, would significantly fewer people join, or would the same number sign up and give more?

Lack of awareness

A further problem is the apparent lack of awareness of the scheme. Even when a company is signed up to a scheme, unless it is well promoted (either by the employer, or charities, or PFOs going into the work place), many employees are often unaware of the existence of the scheme.

The government's dedicated payroll giving campaign is specifically aimed at raising awareness and take-up. Many charities, however, believe it is the responsibility of employers to raise the profile of payroll giving as part of their corporate community investment (CCI) programme. Many companies would agree with this and actively promote schemes, some even offering 'matched giving' initiatives whereby the company will match some or all of employee contributions. However, many companies believe it is the role of charities to promote their causes through the workplace, and feel that they are 'doing their bit' by providing the schemes for their employees.

Role of agency charities

What of the role of payroll-giving agencies? How active should they be in promoting giving campaigns within organisations, once they have encouraged employers to participate? Unlike beneficiary charities, agency charities do not have fundraisers. Agency charities claim the tax back from the government, maintain payroll-giving accounts and distribute payroll donations to charities. The agency charities charge an administration fee of around 4 per cent to cover these costs.

The level of agency charity charges is an issue for some charities and donors. Clearly agencies need to work as transparently and cost-effectively as possible, and competition has produced some downward pressure. On the other hand, the amount of work involved in the tax recovery of hundreds of thousands of individual payments can easily be underestimated by those not doing it, and comes at a cost.

A criticism of agency charities is the amount of time it takes for the donations to reach charities. There has always been a maximum amount of time (a disbursement period), set down by the IR, that an agency can hold on to donations before passing them over to charities. Prior to the 2000 Budget, the disbursement period was 90 days; following the Budget, this was reduced to 60 days. This will inevitably speed up the disbursement process.

Children's Promise Millennium Campaign

The Children's Promise Millennium Campaign was a one-off campaign at the end of 1999 whereby employees were encouraged to donate their last hour's pay of the millennium to a consortium of seven British children's charities. It is similar in many respects to US-style payroll giving, where companies launch annual workplace giving campaigns, with donations directed to a specific charity or charities, often chosen by the employees.

The initiative was conceived by the New Millennium Experience Company and developed in partnership with Marks and Spencer. The payroll-giving figures for the year 2000/01 show income from payroll giving had reached £55 million. In all, £8 million was raised, a figure which indicates that other annual, specifically directed campaigns of this type may revitalise payroll giving in Britain.

The future for payroll giving

Undoubtedly, payroll-giving schemes have huge potential, if their particular benefits can be widely understood and their operation made more efficient. What will motivate companies and their employees to get involved?

Many believe that endorsement by business leaders would encourage take-up. Should it be mandatory for employers to offer their employees the opportunity to receive the benefits of payroll-giving schemes?

If access to payroll-giving schemes were seen as part of corporate social responsibility, or even as a condition of a quality standard such as the *Investors in People* award, would this encourage employers to promote their payroll-giving schemes regularly to their employees?

Finally, the spotlight falls on charities themselves. What role should charities play in promoting payroll giving in the workplace? Should charities be more actively involved in going into the workplace to promote schemes, and encourage employees to regularly support their cause through the payroll?

If payroll giving in Britain is to achieve the status and success of its transatlantic cousin, there is clearly much work to be done – by charities, employers and payroll-giving agencies – to raise its profile and the level of participation. With the charity tax changes, there has never been a better time to give through the payroll – it is an opportunity too good to miss.

A case study of payroll giving in the Bank of England, which illustrates some of the issues that the scheme needs to address, is given below (see pp 96–8).

TAXING TIMES IN A BRAVE NEW WORLD? OPPORTUNITIES AND DIFFICULTIES POSED BY THE MILLENNIUM TAX CHANGES   Mark Robson

The evidence given so far in this chapter has indicated that individuals and charities could gain more from charity tax reliefs than they do. This note explores:

*   some of the reasons why the take-up of tax-effective giving might be low;
*   whether and how the new arrangements may make a difference;
*   whether these new arrangements introduce any new difficulties for charity donors or for donees.

But to set these changes in context, it is first useful to review some recent history of charities and taxation. My argument is that there has been a clear shift, if only as an accidental by-product of the main thrust of government policy, encouraging charities to switch from reliance on investment income to active pursuit of donor funding.

Dividend tax credits

Prior to the Charities Tax Review, the most significant policy change to have affected any charities with investment income from financial capital (including many of the smaller and older foundations) was the announcement in Chancellor Brown's first budget of July 1997 that dividend tax credits were to be abolished.

Just as the earlier reduction in the dividend tax credit in 1993 was phased out by Norman Lamont over four years for charities, this further blow was cushioned by phasing out from 1999 to 2004. The position over the decade is nevertheless a sorry one for charities relying heavily on investment income to support their expenditure, as Table 5.10 indicates.

Of course, the motivation for this policy change was to affect the incentives of pension-fund trustees to require, and companies to pay, dividends, not to deprive charities of a large part of their income. But nevertheless, a dividend of £750 topped up to £1,000 in 1992 will by 2004 have become just a dividend of £750.

On top of that bad news, since the main motivation for the change

Table 5.10 Charities and taxation of dividends from British companies

Year	Corporation tax rate (%)	Percentage of dividend repayable (%)	Tax credits paid to charities (£m)
1990–91	34	33	169
1996–97	33	25	288
1997–98	31	25	237
1998–99	31	25	173
1999–2000	30	21	264
2000–01	30	17	199
2001–02	30	13	?
2002–03*	? 30 ?	8	?
2003–04*	? 30 ?	4	?
2004–05*	? 30 ?	–	Prior years only

Source Inland Revenue Statistics, 2000.

*We do not yet know the corporation tax rates up to 2005, nor of course the tax credits that will actually be paid in those years – but we do know that the transitional relief for charities will run out by April 2004.

(apart from, obviously, raising more tax revenue) was to 'remove a distortion in the tax system which encourages the distribution of profits as dividends rather than their retention and reinvestment', the rate of dividends paid out to investors by companies could fall too. There is already some evidence for this effect. The only consolation might be higher capital gains; but the very poor performance of the FTSE markets at the end of 1999 and the beginning of 2000 may have encouraged charity trustees to consider switching their investments from equity to debt, the relative attractiveness of which has increased – since, unlike dividends, interest is still receivable on a gross basis.

The change to dividend taxation will wipe out income from repayable tax credits that, at its height in 1996/97, immediately before the announcement, amounted to no less than £288 million –

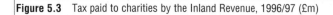

Figure 5.3 Tax paid to charities by the Inland Revenue, 1996/97 (£m)

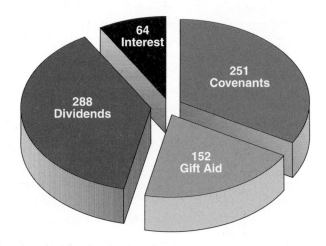

easily the largest component of the taxman's charity cheque (see Figure 5.3).

Not just the tax relief but also the investment income itself of charities is shrinking fast, apparently reflecting both lower dividend payouts and interest rates.

To maintain the same level of expenditure, charities need to be increasingly resourceful in fundraising. Fortunately, the level of covenants – and strikingly, the level of Gift Aid payments – has been rising fast.

Some old problems that do not go away (and may well get worse)

As has been noted, the main vehicles for tax benefits through donor funding are covenants and the Gift Aid scheme. Covenants are big business for many British charities. As at the last CAF survey (Pharoah and Street, 2001), three charities had covenant income into seven figures at the end of the 1990s: the National Trust at £55.7 million, Action Aid at £22.7 million and World Vision UK at £12.0 million. Since the basic rate of income tax has declined over the last two decades, the value to such charities of a net contribution of a given size has evidently fallen (relief for higher rates of tax benefiting the giver rather than the charity). But the great advantage of the covenant relief in the past was the fact that charities could use it to secure a more stable stream of income. Certainly before the introduction of Gift Aid, an individual offering a particular sum of money as a one-off payment could be encouraged to help the charity further by donating the same sum indefinitely or at least for a further three years; or, if that did not work, by spreading it as a deposited covenant to be released in four annual instalments. The Inland Revenue had no objection to the latter practice, perhaps because the necessary documentation could only enhance the available audit trail.

Now that approach is no longer relevant. A single payment of any size suffices for a Gift Aid donation, and covenants will simply die out (not least because company donations can now all be made gross of tax). The total amount of covenanted payments fell sharply, from £1,325 million in 1999/2000, to £850 million in 2000/01.

There are, however, long-standing difficulties with ensuring that the qualifications for relief are made by Gift Aid payments. These may well become more difficult to avoid and to police as the volume of such payments increases enormously.

The first of these concerns the need to establish and retain adequate records. The former Gift Aid certificate is abolished for companies and replaced for individuals by a much more straightforward form of declaration. The charity establishes as a minimum the name and address of the donor and the payments that are to be treated as Gift Aid donations (the significance of that being that, if the donor is not a taxpayer, he or she must be prepared to pay the tax that the charity is going to claim).

In principle, this system could apply to the smallest donations given to street corner or door-to-door collectors (particularly since, in the latter case, the address is in most cases pretty obvious). The charity has an incentive, as long as the donor is a taxpayer, to collect the basic-rate tax; higher-rate donors have an incentive to collect the difference between higher- and basic-rate tax. The key question is whether the extra effort is worth it, but the answer depends critically on the standard of record keeping that the Revenue will require on inspection and audit. The official advice (IR, 1998) on inspections predates the new scheme and is in any event in rather general terms; it is now amplified a little by *Guidance Notes for Charities* (IR, 2000), which explains the record-keeping requirements. But we do not yet know what the Revenue will require as an acceptable standard in practice.

The great advantage of the Gift Aid scheme as originally devised was that the gifts had to be sufficiently large that there would almost always be an automatic audit trail for the payment. Gifts were unlikely to have been made in cash. Now the reverse is true, and most payments (by volume) certainly will be in small change or notes.[3]

There are ingenious software packages designed to help charities recover tax on Gift Aid donations from 'bob a job' and 'sponsored swim'-type appeals involving children, but will the typical donor and donee manage to cope with all this bureaucratic apparatus effectively year after year? Moreover, a potentially serious complication arises from the interaction of Gift Aid at the basic rate to the charity and higher-rate relief to the donor. A sadly over-organised individual might be able to rely on his meticulously kept record of payments to defend his claim to personal relief at 18 per cent (ie 40 per cent less 22 per cent). But if the charity's records contain no mention of a cash receipt from him, and no claim to the basic-rate tax, who should be believed? Of course, he could demand a receipt from the collector, but this is so far from the successful and popular world of street corner tin rattling as to defy belief.

A similar problem has existed for several years with 'benefits' potentially provided by the charity for the donor, which may disqualify a claim for tax relief (see Ghosh and Robson, 1993). Unfortunately the test is whether such benefits (typically, free or reduced cost of admission to exhibitions or events or publications) are available for the donor, not whether he or she is able to take advantage of them, or in fact does so. If the potential value of the

---

[3] *I asked a senior IR official how he felt that charities collecting on street corners should approach this, and he told me, entirely seriously, that he always carried around a small notebook just for the purpose of recording his donations, and a small supply of Gift Aid declarations with his name and address pre-printed!*

benefits exceeds the *de minimis* threshold,[4] then higher-rate tax relief is denied. Yet the donor has no control over whether benefits are offered or not – it is a matter for the charity alone.

It is therefore questionable whether the nature of the original Gift Aid scheme, devised for large payments other than cash, is really suitable to be extended down to every single cash donation to charities. Is it now 'fit for purpose'?

Gifts of shares and securities

The new income tax benefits on gifts of shares and securities may not apply to more than a small proportion of the population, apart from those that acquired small amounts of demutualisation shares and may be fed up with them in a bear market. There is clear evidence of take-up in the first year of operation, and it is being actively promoted by certain organisations such as the Community Foundation Network, CAF, and the Giving Campaign. Early reports indicate that some charities find it difficult to administer, and individuals are likely to need expert help in compliance with the rules. The scheme may be particularly useful for wealthy individuals with share options to exercise, or a significant stake in a business they have built up and subsequently floated. In that case, the charity will usually have to sell the shares in order to comply with a prudent, diversified investment policy.

Payroll giving

Adopting precisely the opposite approach to Gift Aid, payroll giving was introduced from 1987 with a very low annual maximum on relief, initially only £120, and has therefore been described as a 'blue collar' scheme.

What have been the problems with payroll giving that make the take-

---

[4] *The* de minimis *concession exempts charities from paying income tax where the overall total trading income of the charity is no greater than £5,000 or the lesser of £50,000 and 25 per cent of the charity's gross income. Since April 2000 the procedure for assessing the tax status of benefits has become bewilderingly complex. Tax relief is denied if that value exceeds 25 per cent of total gifts in the year to the same charity up to £100; £25 if the gifts total between £100 and £1,000; and 2.5 per cent if they exceed £1,000; and this presupposes that the value of the potential benefits is known by the donor (which, in many cases, it will not be).*

up still so relatively disappointing? Evidently the scheme started out far too cautiously, but that was also the case with personal equity plans and performance-related pay, both of which took off in a striking way once the early constraints were relaxed. Payroll giving has specific challenges. It is available only to employees and occupational pensioners whose employers feel it is worth the bother to offer and administer through the payroll. So the self-employed, personal pensioners, unemployed persons and employees with uninterested employers do not even get a look in. But that still leaves a very large number of potential payroll givers, and, without any upper limit at all, the total amount donated through this mechanism could become very large indeed.

An informal case study of payroll giving in practice, at the Bank of England

At the Bank of England, as indeed with many City firms, there is a long history of very generous fundraising by staff, both for large national charities and small local ones, often initiated by a member of staff and associated with a personal commitment, such as the disability of a family member or friend. The Bank as employer makes grants of up to £500 to complement the time commitment of each employee to charitable or community organisations, donates spontaneously to many good causes and matches the donations of employees through the payroll-giving scheme. So there is a very strong institutional culture of supporting charities.

This has not yet extended to payroll giving. Prior to the national relaunch in October 2000, only 52 current staff (out of about 2,000) and 115 pensioners were participating, and the total level of donations had remained stable at about £60,000 for five years. Now the number of current staff has risen to 86 and the level to £70,000. It is important to look at what might be inhibiting enthusiasm. Views expressed by staff who strongly support charities are revealing. Payroll deductions are seen to have generally an unwelcome association: with income tax, national insurance, loan repayments (now including student loans), attachment orders for some. For most people, charitable giving evidently does not fit happily in this list. Some would not want their employer or the colleagues administering the payroll to know to which charities they were giving, or how much per month. The first of these objections is of course easily dealt with in the 'umbrella' account schemes operated by CAF and others, which provide all the flexibility and anonymity one could reasonably want. But, even if this is pointed out, the amount given was a problem. Some generous middle managers were concerned that, if it were known that a large proportion of them gave a significant amount to charity, this could affect their prospects in the annual pay round. This could also be the case for smaller private-sector employers in particular: 'With the business facing hard times, if X can afford to give 10 per cent of his income to charity, he certainly doesn't need a 3 per cent pay rise this year.' There appears to be some feeling that disposal of income should be separated from the source – just as most of us would not be very happy if our employer proposed to settle our credit card bills directly out of our salary. Ways of addressing this need to be explored

Similarly, many staff felt that they would rather their charitable giving remained entirely spontaneous. They were very happy to give generously when asked directly, and tax efficiency was a second-order consideration. But, given the universal availability of Gift Aid, they were even less likely to consider the rather clinical and calculating method of payroll giving. This suggests that alternative incentive schemes, as they are now constructed, might work against each other at the margin. In the past, it was clear that payroll giving was for regular small donations, and Gift Aid was for occasional, perhaps rare, large ones. If this analysis is correct, it explains why the additional 10 per cent 'top-up', necessarily provided out of public expenditure rather than as a tax deduction,[5] is required to persuade employees to adopt the pattern of regular rather than always spontaneous giving with marginal tax relief under the Gift Aid scheme.

Unfortunately, complexity in the administration of tax-effective giving remains due in part to the fact that Gift Aid and payroll giving are quite different. Such complexity is a general feature of what has happened to the tax system since 1997. But tax payment is

---

[5] *In very unusual tax legislation, because 'the Board [of Inland Revenue] shall pay out of money provided by Parliament', the amount of which is evidently completely unknowable in advance: section 38, Finance Act 2000.*

compulsory; charitable donation is not, and, as a matter of the sensible design of policy, government support should be given as transparently as possible. Simplification, a brighter image and promotion of the benefits of regular committed payments to charities might all enhance the success of payroll giving. The 10 per cent supplement and the government's promotional campaign already appear to be having positive effects.

To what does it all add up?

After only one year of the new tax regime, it is too early to assess how significant a difference it will make to the financial situation of charities in raising funds from taxpayers – or, more dramatically, to the approach and attitude to the role of British charities in our national and international life. More money has been raised through Gift Aid and payroll giving than before, and that is very welcome, but there has been no dramatic qualitative change in giving yet. More broadly, the Exchequer will be watching the overall tax cost of the implementation of the new reliefs.

The current strategy relies, it appears, on taxpayers thinking to themselves 'For every pound of net income I give, the charity will receive so much more; so how much shall I give and to which charities?' In reality, people are more likely to consider how much they think that they can reasonably afford; and then, usually at the charity's prompting (although some of our largest and most prominent charities are very poor at this), the gift may become tax-effective.

It may not be appropriate to rely only on tax reliefs to individuals to generate extra charity income. This point has long been made: for the USA, by Burt Weisbrod and others;[6] most recently, in the UK, by Banks and Tanner. Given the spontaneous nature of much giving, government could say to charities 'Go out and fundraise, and whatever you obtain next year from any sources whatsoever, we will increase by Z per cent as a government grant'. Traditionally there have been obscure parliamentary problems with giving money out as public expenditure rather than tax reliefs, but this hurdle has

---

[6] *Weisbrod (1986) contains an excellent review of the evidence and arguments.*

evidently been easily overcome for the 10 per cent payroll-giving top-up.

What might the advantages of this quite different approach be? First, it would remove the rather invidious distinction between tax-paying givers and non-tax-paying givers that arises under Gift Aid. Second, it would deal with the problem that payroll giving is obviously available only to employees whose employer chooses to operate the scheme. Third, it would stop the current income tax relief being weighted to individuals with higher incomes and their preferred charities. Fourth, it would greatly reduce the administrative burden, for the Inland Revenue, the charities and the givers. On the other hand, fundraising costs to charities might rise. Further research is needed to determine which approach would raise the most money for charities, in the most cost-effective way.

To sum up, the personal commitment of Chancellor Gordon Brown to help enhance the value of charities' fundraising efforts is very evident. After only the first year of the new millennium reliefs, it is too early to be able to judge whether this policy will be the most effective use of taxpayers' funds. But it is to be hoped that the Chancellor will keep an open mind and be prepared to review the policy in the light of evidence as to how well it is working.

CONCLUSION   Cathy Pharoah

In this chapter, tax-effective giving has been appraised in some detail, and it has been shown that income tax reliefs on individual giving to charities are a very powerful and sophisticated mechanism for increasing charities' income. As with all powerful machines, however, there are challenges both in understanding how they work and in learning how to use them to maximum effect. Sometimes their effects can be unpredictable, and this needs to be taken into account. The rewards of investment in developing tax-effective, planned and regular giving, however, will be great. The last decade has seen governments increasingly keen to support personal giving through the tax system, and some very radical – and increasingly experimental – adaptations to fiscal measures. The income to charities generated through tax-effective giving mechanisms has increased steadily, and it is clear that tax-effective giving currently offers greater potential for significant new growth over the next decades than any other fundraising technique. The challenge needs to be taken up by charities, fundraisers, financial advisers – and ultimately by donors. The Giving Campaign will make an important contribution to this. Imaginative ways of ensuring that all giving takes place within a tax-effective framework need to be developed; the public needs to be made increasingly aware of the leverage power of their donations.

References

Banks J and Tanner S (1997) *The State of Donation*. London: IFS.

Banks J and Tanner S (1998) *Taxing Charitable Giving*, Commentary 75. London: IFS.

Foster V, Mourato S, Pearce D and Ozdemiroglu E (2000) *The Price of Virtue: the economic value of the charitable sector*. Cheltenham: Edward Elgar.

Ghosh I J and Robson M H (1993) 'Charity and consideration', *British Tax Review*, 1993:6, pp 496–503.

Inland Revenue (1998) 'Code of Practice 5: Inspection of charities records', Inland Revenue External Communications Unit, November 1998. London: Inland Revenue. (available at http://www.inlandrevenue.gov.uk/pdfs/cop5.pdf)

Inland Revenue (2000) 'Guidance note for charities', (Chapter 7 and Appendix F). London: Inland Revenue. (available at http://www.inlandrevenue.gov.uk/charities/index.htm)

Jones P, Cullis J, and Lewis A (1998) 'Public Versus Private Provision for Altruism'. *Kyklos* **51**: 3–24.

Jones A and Posnett J (1991) 'Charitable donations by UK households: evidence from the Family Expenditure Survey'. *Applied Economics* **23**: 343–51.

Office for National Statistics (1996) *Family Resources Survey*. London: Stationer's Office.

Passey A, Hems L and Jas P (2000) *The UK Voluntary Sector Almanac 2000*. London: NCVO.

Pharoah C and Street S (eds) 2001 *Dimensions 2000: an update on CAF's Top 500 Fundraising Charities*. West Malling: CAF.

Weisbrod B A (1986) *The Non-Profit Economy*. Harvard University Press.

Yarmolinsky A (2000) 'The charitable deduction: subsidy or limitation?' *Nonprofit and Voluntary Sector Quarterly* **29**(1).

WHAT MAKES A CAUSE WORTH GIVING TO?   Les Hems

The study of charitable giving behaviour by academics and practitioners is extremely challenging and has until recently been under-resourced both financially and intellectually in Britain. This becomes most apparent after you have scratched the surface and started to discover the immense complexity of the behaviour that is currently conceptualised as charitable giving and of which our understanding is patchy.

Scratching the surface of charitable giving behaviour

Much attention has been paid to the scale of charitable giving by the general public, its significance in terms of British voluntary sector activity – a fifth of the total current income of all British general charities – and its significance in the bigger picture of the economy, charitable giving having much the same volume of consumer expenditure as another 'national institution', the National Lottery.

During the mid-1990s, attention focused on an apparent decline in charitable giving and participation. In the latter half of the 1990s, this attention shifted to the lack of growth in charitable giving at a time when the economy was strong and charitable causes remained in the foreground of daily life. A number of explanations have been put forward for the decline and lack of growth, including:

* the possibly negative impact of the National Lottery – a substitute or competing good?
* the long-term decline in giving observed in successive generations of young households (Banks and Tanner, 1997);
* a decline in the general public's trust in some major public institutions (the significance of which for charities is dealt with later in this chapter by Andrew Passey).

These explanations were no doubt important contextual factors for the Charities Tax Review and influential in the introduction of enhanced mechanisms for tax-effective giving that were initially targeted at specific causes – Millennium Gift Aid. Figures towards the end of the 1990s indicate a reversal of the downward trend in levels of giving and a climb back to, or just above, the levels seen in the early 1990s (NCVO/NOP 2001). Participation levels, however, are continuing to drop.

Most recently, attention has shifted to international comparisons, specifically with the USA, where comparisons on a per capita or GDP basis reveal much lower levels of giving in the UK – around 0.6 per cent in the UK compared with around 2 per cent in the USA. The UK's 'philanthropic deficit' is now a powerful driver for generic initiatives to promote charitable giving, such as the Giving Campaign – the assumption being that there is considerable latent potential for increasing charitable giving.

Understanding the complexity – the differential impact of the decline in charitable giving

The general public supports an extremely diverse range of causes. Some causes are defined by beneficiary, such as young people or children; other causes are defined by activity, such as medical research. Both of these types of cause are supported by one in five givers. Table 6.1 provides a categorisation of causes which, although over-simplifying the immense diversity of charitable activity, may nevertheless highlight the 'democracy of giving'.

The impact of the decline in charitable giving on charities in the mid-1990s was not uniform. Religious, health and social care organisations, for example, rely particularly heavily on charitable giving (Passey et al, 2000, Table 3.11). The NCVO/NOP consumer research programme suggests that planned giving and large-scale donations by the general public were not affected, the most notable change in behaviour relating to small-scale spontaneous or loose-change giving.

A comparison of the causes supported by 'elite givers' – those who give £50 or more a month – and 'other givers' is most revealing (see

Table 6.1 The level of support for different causes by proportion of all givers supporting each cause (%)

Beneficiary causes (%)		Activity causes (%)		Other (%)	
Children or young people	19.2	Medical research	21.6	Animals	9.9
Elderly people	7.6	Overseas aid and development	10.6	Environment	1.7
Disabled people	7.5	Medical care	10.5	Heritage	0.8
Blind people	5.6	Religion	10.4		
Homeless people	5.5	Rescue services	5.2		
Deaf people	1.8	Education	1.9		
		Arts, music, culture	0.7		

Source Passey et al, (2000, Table 3.5).

Table 6.2). Almost half (43.4 per cent) of elite givers support religious organisations, compared with only one in ten (10.7 per cent) of 'other givers'. The same proportion of elite givers (43.3 per cent) support children or young people, compared with one in five of other givers (21.2 per cent). And almost one in three elite givers (29.9 per cent) support international aid and development, compared with less than one in ten (8.5 per cent) other givers. The causes least supported by 'other givers' are culture, arts and music (0.8 per cent) and heritage (0.75 per cent). When comparing the mean amounts given, elite givers donate seventy-five times as much to heritage (£1.88 compared with £0.02), and thirty-eight times as much to culture, arts and music (£1.39 versus £0.04).

The British philanthropic deficit

Seeking explanations for the British philanthropic deficit provides an effective vehicle for considering the significance of individual charitable causes and for drawing interesting and illuminating comparisons between components of giving behaviour in the USA and in the UK. Three particular causes attract more giving in the USA

Table 6.2 Causes supported by elite givers and other givers

Cause	Proportion supporting each cause (%)		Mean amounts given (£)	
	Elite givers	Other givers	Elite givers	Other givers
Religion	43.4	10.8	22.03	0.60
Children and young people	43.3	21.2	20.58	0.88
International aid	29.9	8.5	13.06	0.40
Heritage	7.8	0.8	1.88	0.02
Culture, arts and music	5.4	0.8	1.39	0.04

Source NCVO/NOP 2000.

than in the UK, and have much more highly organised fundraising systems. First, 'religious'-based giving is a dominant component of charitable giving. It represents approximately 40 per cent of all giving in the USA, compared with 13 per cent in the UK. It arguably distorts the picture, so there is a strong case for removing religious giving from comparisons and, in effect, treating it as a separate 'behaviour'. If religious charitable giving behaviour were linked exclusively to 'sacramental' activities, then this argument would be defendable. However, in the USA, religious organisations not only undertake sacramental activities but also run considerable social and community programmes, whereas in the UK religious organisations' activities are more exclusively sacramental; typically, UK religious organisations would create separate charitable organisations to undertake social and community activities.

Secondly, another philanthropic activity where the USA and the UK differ markedly is alumni (university) giving, which is very significant in the USA. In comparison, alumni giving in the UK, where it has only recently been pro-actively exploited by university fundraisers, is paltry. Thirdly, in the USA there is a long-established and almost universal mechanism to attract philanthropic resources for local community-based causes – the United Way. Donors can be assured that their donations are applied to their local community without having to determine which causes have priority – the allocation of funds is managed through the sophisticated grant-giving systems constructed by each local United Way. There has been growing interest in such community funds in the UK recently, and in theory local payroll giving schemes could channel funds into them.

Of course, it is important to note that these three cause-related differences between US and UK giving – in religion, university alumni and localities – are closely linked to the different welfare systems and cultural norms of each country.

Giving to causes or giving to institutions, charity brands, events, commodities and localities?

The key question to ask is whether people's charitable giving behaviour is determined by the cause itself or by some other aspects of the 'philanthropic transaction', or process for giving. For example, religious giving is a significant and distinctive component of charitable giving. It could be argued that it is 'faith'-based and habitual, so even in times of declining church attendance the volume of charitable giving to religious institutions remains strong. It is not clear what proportion of this charitable giving is driven by and consumed by sacramental activities and, conversely, what proportion is driven by and is applied to other subsidiary charitable causes.

The philanthropic link with institutions other than religious institutions is most apparent in the USA, where university alumni giving is highly significant. It is possible that this philanthropic behaviour will expand rapidly in Britain over the next few years. This type of institutional link is also apparent from the analysis of the behaviour of elite givers, which showed that elite givers, unlike other givers, support culture, arts and music, and heritage causes. It is likely that the elite givers receive some private benefit in relation to their donations to these causes (patrons to theatres, opera houses, etc) as well as facilitating wider public benefit. These are examples of giving behaviour that are linked to institutions.

The heavy investment in sophisticated communication and fundraising techniques by large charities has made these charities appear synonymous with the cause for which they operate. The power of this strategy is demonstrated through the increasing emphasis on charity branding. A recent interesting example in Britain relates to mental health, where the charity MIND has the brand most synonymous with the cause. Recently Mencap, another leading mental health charity, was facing a 'grassroots rebellion': two local branches complained that the approach of the national charity was outdated. Other charities have chosen to merge similar causes under the strongest and best-known brand name.[1] Some charitable giving behaviour is therefore driven by individual charities or, more specifically perhaps, by charity brands closely identified with causes.

It has also been suggested that charities operating under the auspices of a cause could create or invest in one organisation as an umbrella fundraising vehicle for that cause. This would remove wasteful aspects of competition and ensure clear communication of the cause. This strategy has been adopted in relation to cancer and homelessness, and its efficacy is under close scrutiny by other charities. It is, however, clear that it would require a high level of collaboration, and for some causes this would contrast sharply with the current highly competitive environment.

This collaborative-based strategy has some similarities with media-driven national events such as Children in Need and Comic Relief, which relate to a range of specified causes and benefit a large number of organisations. The question is whether it is the causes or the events that drive charitable giving behaviour. Further, it could be argued that these two events are the sustainable outcomes of the 1985 Live Aid event, which could perhaps be more appropriately called a 'social movement'. In these cases, it is perhaps the attraction of participating in a national media event as much as the causes that drives charitable giving behaviour.

---

[1] *For example, the Terence Higgins Trust merged in 1999 with four regional charities: Bridgeside in Leeds, the HIV Network in Coventry, Sussex Aids Centre in Brighton and OXAIDS in Oxford. In October 2000, they merged with London Lighthouse, making them the largest HIV and AIDS charity in Europe. BBC news online said that the original merger was 'the most complex yet undertaken in the voluntary sector and [one that] may herald a revolution in the way charities are run' (BBC news online, January 1999). (The new charity is still called the Terence Higgins Trust.)*

The decline in trust in public institutions, including charities, has shifted attention from trust- to confidence-based relationships. This shift is exemplified by adaptation of fundraising strategies, especially within certain causes. For example, charitable giving in relation to international aid has traditionally been based on a trust relationship; it is difficult for the donor to assess whether their donation has been applied to the desired cause by the recipient charity. Over recent years, there have been numerous innovative fundraising mechanisms constructed that are based on confidence or contract – philanthropic monetary units related to the provision of units of health care, water, education, etc. Charitable giving behaviour has therefore become more 'commodified', with donors selecting philanthropic 'purchases' rather than just supporting a cause.

Although empathy for a cause is an important driver of charitable giving behaviour, it is not the only one. The desire to apply philanthropic resources locally is also important, reflecting the importance of 'proximity' and 'communities of place' – it may also facilitate the development of trust- and confidence-based relationships. In the USA, the United Way provides an effective vehicle for such philanthropic behaviour (although isolated cases of fraud and malpractice have undermined this method in the past). In the UK, applying philanthropic resources locally is typically done directly with cause-specific organisations that are either independent local organisations or branches of national organisations; as noted above, the emergence of community foundations may provide an opportunity to develop new mechanisms to attract local philanthropic resources.

Conclusion

Strategies designed to close Britain's philanthropic deficit and access any latent philanthropic potential must start by recognising the complexity that underpins charitable giving behaviour, including recognising the significance of causes, institutions, charity brands, events, commodities and localities – in other words, the question of what people actually give to. The next step is to understand the motivations for such behaviour by different types of donor – most notably, elite givers (the *why* question).

FROM MARKETING PRODUCTS TO FUNDRAISING FOR CAUSES   Stephen Lee

One of the major changes in fundraising in the period from the early 1980s to the present day has been the growing professionalism of fundraising practice (defined as perceived effectiveness and technical ability, supported by a range of training courses) – as demonstrated by the uncomfortable alignment between marketing techniques developed in the commercial sector in the 1960s and 1970s, and their application to the fundraising process.

Hand in hand with this growing professionalism, however, there has been an actual decline in giving – or, at best, a stagnation through the same period. A legitimate question to ask, therefore, is what all this increased technical ability has actually achieved. Much has been said about the difference between fundraising and marketing (although there has been precious little proper structured research on the matter), but in fact most fundraisers still do not understand the real nature of the activity that they are engaged in. The dilemma is that donors do, particularly committed donors. And if donors perceive the messages from charities and fundraisers as inappropriate, it is small wonder that there is a coincidence between increasing professionalism and declining participation.

The rush to professionalism

Early in the 1970s, charities and voluntary organisations faced what they perceived as virgin or near-virgin potential donor markets, and they applied some of the more aggressive direct-marketing techniques, which were showing success in industry, directly into the voluntary sector. In effect, they just imposed them on the sector – so there was a huge rise in cold direct-marketing acquisition of donors, and an even bigger rise in off-the-page advertising using coupon response to identify and acquire potential supporters. This reached its peak in the mid-1980s with the relaxation of television advertising techniques, and the ability of charities for the first time to engage in paid-for advertising. Many of the larger charities spent considerable sums developing rather unsuccessful above-the-line, high-profile television adverts and got a very poor return. It was ten years later that organisations like the NSPCC, RNLI and others recognised that they had to apply direct-marketing techniques to television advertisements in order to make them effective as acquisition mechanisms. Even translating donors acquired in this way to long-term donors is much more complex than many people thought. A good example is the donor-acquisition attempts made during the break-up of former Yugoslavia by the British Red Cross and others, who demonstrated great ability on the one hand to elicit an immediate cash donation (albeit fairly low-level: £17–20 on average) with an almost complete inability to translate those individuals on to the regular donor programme.

The problem with the more public up-front marketing techniques is that they were costly to develop. They involved external agencies as well as the growth of in-house marketing departments. The sector became more proficient, and started to copy the commercial sector from which these techniques came. Corporate fundraising, for example, emerged as a distinct marketing mix in its own right, including employee fundraising, corporate trust fundraising, right the way through to cause-related marketing, sponsorship and joint promotions. So complex structures developed, designed in the first instance to serve the interests of the charities and the organisations – not necessarily to serve the needs either of beneficiaries or donors. The sector lost sight of what distinguishes the fundraising from the marketing process.

The failure of fundraising techniques to provide a link between donor and beneficiary

Good fundraising is identifying within organisations the needs that exist to be met in relation to organisational mission and vision, identifying people with similar aspirations and concerns, and linking them as closely as possible to beneficiaries. In effect, fundraisers are effective when they provide a catalyst by which donors can achieve their aspirations.

The concern with technique and marketing proficiency is incompatible with that linking process. Donors regard it as an organic process, not as a technocratic process. Donors need to feel in control, and the dilemma of many of these techniques is that their impact is to produce the opposite effect: donors may see the charity imposing its will upon them. They may see the charity as seeking to intrude into their lives in an uninvited way, and simply to be continually asking them for more and more money. At the point of donation, donors are probably not actually interested in money. If donors start thinking about money, then fundraisers have done their job poorly: they are asking either for the wrong amount (probably too much), or in an intrusive way that in itself creates a sense of obligation. The nature of the media or communication device selected can in itself impose a sense of obligation on the donor and have a huge impact on whether they donate for the first time, or whether they continue to donate and feel committed to particular organisations. Such subtleties simply were not entertained in the early 1970s when the life of direct-marketing programmes (both mail and also off-the-page advertising), inserts and reciprocal mailing grew enormously. What these tactics failed to do was expand the breadth of people willing to engage in committed support to charities and voluntary organisations. At best, they have enabled charities and voluntary organisations that use these marketing techniques to develop further support from existing supporters in a more sophisticated and sensitive way. Overall, however, they have failed to increase the size of the cake in a substantial or lasting way.

One result of the reliance upon these techniques is that the sector has actually become fairly good at marketing in comparison with the commercial sector, particularly in the tough area of acquisition. The major national charities have actually concentrated on the more difficult and costly task of acquiring new donors rather than the relatively easy challenge of retention and development. Yet the marketing literature in the commercial sector shows that it is in retention and ultimately in development that organisations find their real profit. In the same way, it is in retaining and developing donors more effectively that most large and medium-sized charities will find their income yields actually increasing most over the next four to five years. The focus on acquisition has also had the disadvantage of leading to compartmentalisation of telephone promotion teams, direct marketing teams, corporate fundraising teams, and community or regional fundraising teams. Organisations in this country do not invest very heavily in fundraising, and yet the return compares very favourably with the return on investment. Unfortunately, there has been poor public and media understanding of fundraising costs, and this has held back the development of fundraising.

Donor fatigue: myth or reality?

In spite of media hype about donor fatigue, all the empirical evidence would show that, where messages are put to potential donors or existing donors in an efficient and effective way, they respond enormously. Look, for example, at the response rates to the ITV Telethon Trust, Comic Relief, and BBC Children in Need. If there were a high degree of cynicism, such organisations would not have compounded high growth figures over the past decade. There are also examples of major appeals and new causes that have accelerated in terms of giving behaviour – like Breakthrough Breast Cancer Care and Woman Kind. The public relates to these causes and gives its support willingly.

However, it is still the case that 90 per cent of our fundraising elicits and is designed to elicit a short-term response from donors. Added to that, organisations have increasingly fuelled donors' expectations of a benefit back to themselves. This has led to a huge increase in the number and scale of fundraising events of all shapes and sizes, and to the integration into direct marketing incentives of little gifts of benefits. Statistically it seems to work, but has anyone asked donors what they really think about having, for example, a shiny little pen in an envelope? Most donors do not support fundraisers, and they hate techniques per se; many may not really support charities. Donors support causes. Supporting the NSPCC, for example, means trying to get rid of child abuse. Fundraisers have to go back and recognise that it is the cause that is the crucial thing, and develop fundraising products around the cause.

This concentration upon technique has also led organisations to follow the principal segmentation device of financial worth used in the commercial sector, and this may not be so appropriate. Organisations in the voluntary sector do not segment – at all – by the degree of commitment or sacrifice involved in a donor's relationship with their cause. The wealthy should, in fact, be finding it very easy to give, and yet the people who give the highest proportion of their income are in the poorest income segments. Such donors, however, are disregarded, although they show a greater level of commitment and self-sacrifice in relation to the beneficiary and the cause than richer people. (Interestingly, the commercial sector is beginning to see that a narrow focus on financial worth alone has been a very blunt-edged sword for them as well.)

Developing relationships with donors

Relationship fundraising, which developed in this country largely as a result of Ken Burnett's work (1992), took as its central premise the notion that the needs of fundraisers can only be met if they concentrate on the needs of donors in relation to beneficiaries, rather than view people simply as cash cows. The dilemma with the relationship fundraising approach is that it is actually a long-term process, not a short-term fix, which many had believed it to be. Most charities have taken on board the rhetoric, but have not actually changed anything in their approach significantly.

The most important thing for fundraisers and charities to realise is that the techniques and communication mechanisms have nothing at all to do with the fundraising process. They are a means of facilitating that process. Consequently it becomes particularly important for charities, in comparison with the commercial sector, to get the selection of communication processes absolutely right in relation to different target groups. If they do not, the nature of the selection process will in itself lead the fundraising to fail, even if the content of the message is right. Donors will be made to feel and act as charity consumers. They will either bin the communications, or give a small amount of money on a temporary transactional basis and go away feeling either absolved, or, worse still, deeply cynical. They will not really have engaged in the philanthropic essence of the communication, which might otherwise commit them to the organisation.

The process of fundraising is all about getting the content within these techniques right. This issue is related to the way in which charities are branding themselves. A charity brand is not the same as a commercial brand. Where charity brands are based on the cause they are very powerful. The Red Cross emblem, for example, is one of the best-known brands, but it is not a commercial brand. If it were imbued with commercialised sentiment, emotion and content, it would probably be seen in a very different fashion. But probably some of the more non-mechanistic elements that constitute charity brands, and that make them so powerful, are more important than they are in the commercial sector, and more important therefore if charities get them wrong. These are elements such as trust and confidence, belief in the organisation, and a sense of idealism, reflecting the individual's attitude towards philanthropy, which are symbolised within the brand of the organisation. These cannot be simply translated from the commercial sector.

There is another element that fundraisers have forgotten, and that is the importance of the normative as opposed to the empirical relationship that donors want to have with causes of their choice. There has been a renewed sense of spiritualism both through the major religions but also through the environmental movement, and a new interest in ethics – that is, wanting to be connected with organisations that are seen to be doing and reflecting the right things. Yet, such public ethical concerns in relation to charities in general, their governance and their service provision have very largely taken a back seat in the last two decades, and they have certainly taken a back seat in the promulgation and the implementation of marketing skills and techniques in the fundraising process.

Satisfaction is nowhere near as important a determinant in driving commitment and loyalty in the voluntary as in the commercial sector, because donor satisfaction is very different from satisfaction within the commercial sector. Charities report back to donors all the time, but what they do is simply express gratitude for a donation, and then often ask for more. They need to find out the degree to which existing donors want, and feel happy about, the communications that they receive from their charities. The degree to which the charity can show expertise and excellent judgement in its service to the beneficiary is a measure of the satisfaction the donor can get from seeing what their gift has achieved. Animal adoption schemes work well because they provide that satisfaction, that link direct to the donor in relation to the consumption of the gift by the beneficiary. There is something in those relationships, therefore, that organisations need to apply in a different way to all fundraising. It is the reason why organisations like UNICEF and the NSPCC, to some extent, have committed to major donor development programmes in which they have actually taken major donors out into the field and enabled them to see the difference their donation makes to the beneficiary. Such donors become powerful ambassadors for the organisation; they become not only people who give in a much more committed way themselves, but advocates to go out and get others to give. This is fantastic marketing, but fundamentally it is also good fundraising. Larger, technocratically driven organisations with huge databases have a much bigger problem in making this a practical reality than the medium and small-scale ones.

The future relationship between charities and donors

What messages emerge from this for charities and their fundraisers? The major challenges facing the sector over the next few decades will be to:

* get to grips with the fundraising process;
* build trust and confidence with the public;
* target people in the way they want to be targeted;
* locate individual giving in a local context, whatever 'local' means to the donor;
* increase donors' satisfaction by connecting them to the impact of their gifts, and, through this satisfaction, to inspire commitment and loyalty.

THE IMPORTANCE OF THE PUBLIC'S TRUST AND CONFIDENCE IN CHARITIES   Andrew Passey

While an emphasis on fundraising methods highlights practical ideas for improving the public's regard for charities, it does not deal with an underlying tension in public attitudes. The problem is that, although charities are legitimised by the *causes* they exist to serve, they are also often undermined by some of the *fundraising* they undertake to resource their activities. This dual public perception is combined with an increasingly sceptical media and a public awareness of charities that is largely limited to a small number of 'brands' (Future Foundation, 2001). The result is that it is easy for 'charities in general' to become tarred with the brush of financial impropriety or excessive administration costs. During such episodes, public attention shifts from the ends of voluntary action (causes) towards the means of funding charities. I would therefore like to think about charitable causes in two ways: first, to distinguish causes in general from specific organisations; and, secondly, to discuss specific types of cause, such as young people, animals, or historic buildings.

By contrasting causes with charities it is possible to inflect the debate over public attitudes in a number of ways. Public trust lies at the root of attitudes to charities, and helps maintain public goodwill in a broad sense. In turn, this provides charities with a political licence to operate, which enables them to out-punch their economic weight. Trust is also a resource that helps charities to win a share of public time and money in competition with other types of agency. However, public trust in charities is not a 'given', and can quickly be eroded and irreparably damaged. What routes, therefore, might charities navigate in order to build and maintain trust in the choppy waters of public opinion?

Trust in the ends, distrust in the means

One starting point is a more nuanced understanding of public attitudes towards institutions in general. Various media have recently reported through their own surveys that the public has less 'confidence' in political parties than a generation previously, that 'trust' is placed in fewer and fewer agencies, and that 'respect' for many public institutions is worryingly low. Attitudes like trust, confidence and respect are run into one another and used interchangeably, as if they meant the same thing. There is, however, good evidence that they do not (Seligman, 1997; Tonkiss and Passey, 1999), and a more subtle appreciation of why they do not can shed light on how organisations might better manage relations with key stakeholders.

Trust and confidence in particular have distinct characteristics:

> One means of thinking about this problem is in terms of a
> distinction between trust – as pertaining to ethical relations

which are not conditioned by an external framework of controls – and confidence – referring to relations which are secured by contract or other regulatory forms, and which proceed on the basis of rational expectations.
(Tonkiss and Passey, 1999)

If we adopt such a distinction, then public trust is connected to the core ethos and social objectives of charities, whereas relations of confidence depend on organisational characteristics such as efficiency in delivering services or providing detailed financial and operational information to stakeholders. In simple terms, we arrive at a distinction between values and institutions, which lies at the core of public attitudes to charities.

A distinction between trust and confidence, while primarily an analytical tool, does have an empirical sense too: surveys suggest the public tends to have more trust in charities than it does confidence (NCVO, 1998). What is more, there is an empirical basis to our distinction between values and institutions. A 1997 NCVO Third Sector Foresight survey revealed that, although 90 per cent of the public respected what charities are trying to do, and 70 per cent agreed that one of the most important thing about charities is the values they hold, more than half (56 per cent) agreed they sometimes felt pressurised into giving to charities. One in three claimed that professional fundraising put them off charities (NCVO, 1998).

We can combine these two variables on fundraising to form two clusters of individuals: those raising concerns over charity fundraising and those explicitly unconcerned. Both groups comprise around 20 per cent of the population – the balance is made up of people not expressing an opinion about either of these fundraising issues, or giving mixed responses. When we compare the characteristics of each group, we see that both have a majority of givers and a gender balance tipped in favour of women (see Table 6.3). The biggest differences are apparent in the amounts they donate (the average among the *unconcerned* being twice that of the *concerned*), in social class and education (almost half of the *unconcerned* coming from social classes ABC1, and more than 20 per cent having received higher education) and in age (the *unconcerned* are markedly younger).

Table 6.3 Comparison of characteristics of members of public who are concerned and unconcerned about fundraising

	Concerned	Unconcerned
Proportion giving (%)	62	66
Proportion female/male (%)	54/46	52/48
Average monthly donation	£7.24	£15.91
Proportion social class ABC1 (%)	39	48
Proportion with higher education (%)	11	21
Proportion aged below 45 (%)	40	57

The intriguing finding is that, although participation in charitable giving is broadly similar between the two groups, the size of donation varies markedly. The question remains over the differential impacts of age, social class, and education on both attitudes to charities and also the level of charitable giving. However, even this brief discussion suggests that charities face challenges as organisations in building and maintaining public support. At the heart of this is a public focus on the means of funding voluntary action, as opposed to the ends.

One response would be to shift this gaze away from organisations and onto specific causes – building bridges between the public and the beneficiary. Is there any relationship between concerns over fundraising and the support (or not) for particular causes? Looking again at our *concerned* and *unconcerned* categories, we observe that both clusters share the same top three causes: children/young people, medical research, and religious organisations. Such a finding probably reflects the degree of fundraising around such causes. However, some interesting differences then emerge: the *unconcerned* are more likely to favour the causes of disadvantaged people both in Britain and overseas, and be less interested in animals (see Table 6.4).

Table 6.4   Top 10 causes of members of public who are concerned about fundraising, cross-ranked with those unconcerned about fundraising

	Concerned	Unconcerned
Children/Young people	1	1
Medical research	2	2
Religious organisations	3	3
Animals	4	7
Disabled people	5	4
Other medical/Health care	6	8
Elderly people	7	10
Rescue services (eg lifeboats)	8	13
Disadvantaged or homeless people in Britain	9	6
Third World/Famine relief overseas	10	5

Managing the conflicts between trust and confidence

So, can charities fundraise in ways that build both trust and confidence? A new form of fundraising, or at least a new twist on the old faithful of street collections, provides an intriguing example of how charities might manage potentially conflicting relations of trust and confidence. Street collections, in which charity volunteers collect the 'loose change' of the public in a spontaneous way, remain one of the most common means of charity fundraising – 24 per cent of British people gave to one in 2000, and the average Briton donated £4.56 that same year. So, how then can we explain the emergence of highly professional groups of fundraisers in several central London streets? They are not interested in your loose change; instead they aim to have you sign up to a longer-term commitment to the particular charity whose name is emblazoned on their fluorescent bibs. As you pass by, they will smile, ask if you have a minute for Charity X, look you in the eye as you converse, and attempt to answer your questions. In short, they are doing what many do in social gatherings – forging new relationships. It is much easier to build trust face to face than via the cold approach of the mailshot.

Once you express an interest and hand over your details, then organisational measures – data protection, asking for your support at appropriate amounts, not asking too often, transparency in feeding back how your gift has been used – kick in to build confidence in your values-based relationship with Charity X. This is a simple lesson in how to exploit a charitable unique selling proposition (shared values via a cause) in order to kick-start a profitable long-term relationship that eventually combines confidence with trust.

RELATING TO NEW DONORS   Stephen Pidgeon

Statistics, population trends and demographic indicators can be baffling. In spite of apparently irrefutable evidence, need the inferences drawn be so black and white? For example, a marketing presentation once described the target audience in definitive terms – the market is male, 40–55, AB and C1 and so on. The market for this product was much broader than that, of course. It was simply that the presenter had failed to point out that, although there were bigger groups of customers with other characteristics, this group (male, 40–55, etc) was statistically over-represented when compared with the British population as a whole and offered interesting marketing challenges. Other audiences were very profitable, but this group made a special marketing effort potentially very rewarding.

Undoubtedly there are changes in the way British donors are supporting charities and, unless fundraisers are nimble on their feet, they will not get the public support that is essential to their work. But let us not get too carried away with statistical trends. Nearly everybody in Britain can be moved to support a charity; it is more a question of how this can be done cost-effectively and in a manner likely to create long-term support. (Adrian Sargeant takes this up in more detail in Chapter 8.)

Keeping traditional donors

While donor profiles are changing, there are still large numbers of traditional donors in their 60s, 70s and 80s who were brought up in a culture where supporting a charity was a duty as well as a pleasure. Moreover, most have now given up their voluntary work and can only support through small cash gifts and legacies. Radical changes in marketing approach will alienate those loyal donors just when they are likely to be most valuable, and on the point of leaving a long-promised legacy. That would not be clever!

But it seems to be harder nowadays than it used to be to engage even this traditional donor – Dorothy Donor. The reasons are obvious. There are many more charities using mass-marketing techniques for their fundraising. The potential audience, although large, is still finite, and the methods used by charities have not changed in 15 years. In the mid-1980s, when these mass-marketing techniques took off, you had to do little more than send an appealing picture, a request for support and a donation form for the money to roll in. That is not how it works now.

So before they do anything else, charities in the first decade of this century will have to look much harder at the way they engage the traditional audience. Because this is the generation possibly most motivated to leave legacies, and because the value of legacy income swamps any other potential mass-marketing income, these donors have to be the first and single most important task for fundraisers.

Such a strategy only sorts out the next twenty years, however, and statistics, psychographics, demographics and every other '–ics' available to us show a depressing trend of non-engagement of the next giving generation.

Capturing new generations of donors

To understand how to engage the next giving generation, you have to look at the changing market environment. Look, for example, at challenges from everyday life. You have to prepare a full-blown dinner party for ten friends. The first thing you do is reach for paper and pencil and list what you have to do: plan the menu, buy the food, do the cooking, choose the wine, clean the house, lay the table and so on. It is a military operation, with the cooking alone probably taking most of the day of the dinner party. Yet, weekly, TV viewers are told that these things are done in the space of a 30-minute programme.

There are other examples. If you played in a band as a youngster, and practised for years in cold garages to achieve the highpoint in your performing career – an appearance at your local school fundraising gig – the thought of 'making it big' was about as real as flying to the moon. But, no problem, it was a major part of your life for a good ten years and you met friends who lasted a lifetime. On TV, bands are now made in 15 weeks, and their first single goes to Number One in the charts immediately.

Or stars are created from nothing at all after a week or two in a hothouse with more cameras than interesting conversations. They have agents, appearance schedules and star-studded smiles moments after having been just ordinary people like you and me.

Everyone will have a personal example. Hear'Say's first record went straight to Number One. I felt I had been involved in their creation, as my family and I had gathered round the TV, choosing who was going to make the band. It had caught our imagination. With very little investment we had got real pleasure out of the process. It was immediate and rewarding. So what is happening, and is it important? Life is experienced as so much more 'instant and immediate' than in the past.

People expect quick results. But is that not what is played on when people are offered the chance to support charities? They read mail shots or watch TV ads, they make their gift (it is only a small gift, whatever 'small' might be in their terms), and they feel good about it. Fundraisers have done what they should be good at: they have engaged the public's imagination and the public has responded with a gift.

It is nice to think the two processes are different, that the gift to our charity is on some higher plane because it will achieve real benefit, while the other is peripheral entertainment. But the reality is that the process is the same – imagination caught and simple pleasure taken. You could argue that this is a recent shift in our culture to more peripheral relationships, the need for instant response and so on. Actually, it is simply that the media are now doing what good charities have been doing for years, but they are now doing it a lot better than charities are.

Going for the long haul

And there is another area where the commercial world is rapidly encroaching on the charity area, potentially posing a threat. The level of the threat is apparent only if you understand the nature of the relationship between a charity and a donor. It has been known for some time that charity propositions that are aimed at the imagination alone will engage a donor for a while but will quickly pale. Propositions such as '£12 makes a blind man see' or '£13 fills a Red Cross parcel' will not sustain a long-term relationship.

A longer-term relationship grows when donors' hearts are engaged, and that will only happen when they buy into the charity's core values and trust develops. Recent research from Henley Management College (Lee and Sargeant, 2001) shows that trust accounts for 66 per cent of the variance between those committed to a charity and those not committed. Most charities are both poor and inconsistent at expressing their values, with disastrous consequences for the donor's trust. Yet, somehow, donors seem nonetheless to commit themselves – they are prepared to overlook charities' incompetence for the moment.

Brand power and donors

It is illuminating to look at the recent changes in brand culture in the commercial sector. First, consider the struggles of once-powerful brands such as C&A, Marks and Spencer, or even Barclays Bank. Five years ago, these were seen as the bastions of British society. Now they have either been blown away or are urgently addressing new images and products. We are as likely to bank with Tesco, buying our groceries and utilities there, and maybe soon our car.

Brand leaders from the 1990s, who have seen much of their brand equity disappear, are trading it in for a new suit of clothes. Royal Mail is now Consignia, Andersen Consulting is Accenture, Unigate is Uniq, our gas is delivered by Transco, most of us drink products from Diageo. No doubt the boardrooms had many fine reasons for the changes but, from a marketing point of view, these major companies are looking for new energy in their brands, new customer Trust.

According to Robert Jones (2000), companies now need to establish an emotional connection with the target audience. The brand must offer 'expansive possibilities' so 'Orange, for instance, is about much more than mobile phones; it's about optimism. Sony is about much more than electronics; it's about miniature perfection.' He concludes that people are no longer looking for 'value for money, but values for money'.

But where does that leave charities? The heart is the territory that charities dwell in – that is where they find the long-term commitment that will lead to legacies. No longer do they have it all to themselves; once again, commercial companies are beginning to do it better than they are.

The question must be – is all now lost? Of course not; these are trends, not certainties, and the commercial world will make as many hash-ups as the charity world has done. But the competition is here, and it is here to stay.

Remember just how powerful charities can be if they get it right, particularly with a little luck thrown in. The Salvation Army Christmas 2000 campaign was a tour de force. It was the culmination of several years of brand clarification and development. The images and messages used in the campaign were more consistent, the propositions had come out of careful testing and research, and five media were employed in an integrated campaign.

The overall result on this cold recruitment campaign was over 100,000 new donors recruited, a return of £2.89 for every £1.00 spent, each of the five media with an ROI (return on investment) of nearly 2:1 or more, and individual results – such as the fact that one of the mail packs produced a 9.2 per cent response rate – breaking industry records. So why was this campaign particularly good, considerably more effective than 1999's, which was itself an award winner?

November 2000 was a stressful time for Britain. Floods were devastating many parts of the country; the murders of young Damilola Taylor in an inner-city housing estate and Victoria Climbié at home in the hands of her carers provoked heart-searching questions about the conditions of children in inner-city communities; rail and road travel was nightmarish in the wake of the Hatfield disaster. Britain needed the strength, stability and sheer goodness of the

Salvation Army in operation as a symbol that enough was right in the world to continue in the face of the otherwise bleak news.

That is how powerful a strong charity brand can be. No commercial company could get anywhere near it.

Re-establishing connections to donors

So, does the charity sector have the power to re-establish its position with donors?

Unequivocally, yes. It has the power, but the more difficult question is 'Does it have the vision or the will?' And the answer to that is 'Only in parts!'

The charity sector is obsessed at the moment with structure and process. Fundraisers are under pressure to achieve budgets, of course – nothing wrong with that. But their response is to tackle only the well-proven: reduce spend rather than increase income, never go out on a limb, follow the field.

To look again at our commercial competitors – and competitors they are, for they now see value in tackling the heart as well as the head – they are obsessed with the concept of 'customer relationship management'. Many would say it is not new, it is just good marketing, and they are right. But the difference is that this has caught the interest of the boardroom. Until now, the only thing directors knew about marketing was advertising and only because someone at their next dinner party might ask them about it. Now money is pouring into the strategies and systems that are needed to change corporate culture in favour of the customer.

Charities must have a fundraising vision, not just a strategy. Their vision has to encompass the concept of managing individual relationships, however many individuals that might mean. Only that way will the hearts of their supporters, of whatever demography, be engaged.

Some charities are brilliant at it. Just look at Oxfam's web-centred service for those supporters who sign up to it. Regular e-mails draw attention to what is happening in the world, Oxfam's response to it and what to do about it. There is information on what their donors contributed to, and issues they are concerned about. Speaking for my own experience, very often I do not even look at the e-mails; sometimes I read them all and move on into the website with simple double clicks. It is a fantastic service. And if, occasionally, I respond to the e-mail, there is an immediate answer. I am just one of Oxfam's 500,000 supporters who make regular monthly donations. Yet I feel special.

A charity's fundraising vision must describe that 'specialness'. The fundraising strategy will outline how it will be achieved. For Dorothy Donor, 'specialness' will be achieved through a recognition of what levels of correspondence she is comfortable with, our politeness and interest in her needs. For Susan Donor (now in her 50s and a wholly different character), 'specialness' will come from service levels, quality of information and how it is delivered, and the practical ways she can be helped to give. Neither Dorothy nor Susan will put up with the abuse they have received from many fundraisers over the last 15 years. Why should they? There are enough commercial companies learning how to appeal to their hearts.

Go right back to marketing basics, accepting both that the demography of supporters is changing and that today's 'instant' marketing world is imposing even more pressures to deliver what supporters want. Invest in good technology. Go back and rework fundraising strategy.

The satisfaction of making a difference

The advantage of the commercial world lies in 'satisfaction'. If selling a tangible product results in customer satisfaction, then they will sell more of them. Charities have to create, then sustain, that satisfaction. The product is intangible, with the result that customers usually do not know what they are getting until they do not get it.

But it is so easy to sustain satisfaction in the charity sector. What charities do is hugely exciting, and supporters really want to know they are making a difference. They are up for it. It is fundraisers who may let them down.

The demography of supporters is changing – that is certain. Cathy Pharoah sketches some new donor profiles below. New media, new techniques are now available and must be exploited. But be under no illusion: the fundamental issue remains the same. Fundraising will be successful only when individual donors are engaged in the cause and honoured for that engagement. That requires innovation, risk, detailed analytical work getting to grips with supporters and passion for the cause. It will not be delivered by the application of rules and formulae. It will be hard work, but it will be both financially and emotionally rewarding.

DONOR PROFILING Cathy Pharoah

Future wealth patterns inevitably influence any donor profiling exercise. Recent national income figures show that in 2000 the wealth gap between rich and poor continued to widen. The poorest 20 per cent of households had 6 per cent of national income after tax, while the share held by the top fifth had risen to 45 per cent. How much of this wealth at the top is likely to be shared with charities?

The new income tax relief on gifts of shares and securities to charities might act as an incentive to the new class of share owners in society. In 1998 17 per cent of the population held shares worth £251 billion: demutualisation shares worth £5 billion alone were sold in 1997 and 1998. Already there is considerable evidence of the attractiveness of share giving.

But, if the signs are right about the potential for new giving and new givers, then, as Stephen Pidgeon says above, there is a strong question mark over whether charities know how to attract new groups of donor. Fresh thinking is needed. The figures in Chapter 4 exposed how charities' traditional donors are middle-class, well-educated, and middle-aged. What might the donor profiles of this group look like in the future?

What trends are likely to have the most influence on individual and private giving over the next few decades? Future British society will have a higher proportion of older people; it will be multi-cultural and increasingly polarised in wealth. Work patterns will be more fluid, characterised by mobility and entrepreneurialism. Communications will be increasingly electronic and global. People will seek new networks and identities in an increasingly complex environment. Four possible new donor profiles are sketched out below for charities to include in the 'Wanted' columns of their fundraising strategies.

Woman, living in the South East, middle-class and middle-aged

In 2015, for the first time the number of people aged over 65 will surpass those under 16. Now this should be good news for charities because, while 17 per cent of younger households give to charity, twice as many older households give (34 per cent), and their average weekly donations are 70 per cent larger. So one growth market is apparently the one that the sector has always been good at targeting – the 'middle-aged, middle-class female, living in the South East'.

But she will look quite different. The prime donor pool has been the cohort of middle-class women, encouraged back into the home after World War II, financially dependent on their husbands, socially dependent on their families. They had limited access to education, married young and did not divorce. They experienced increasing leisure time due to technological advances, which they often devoted to charitable work. As well as key donors to charity, they have been a rich source of voluntary labour.

In future, such women will have had good access to higher education, held jobs and been financially independent for a large part of their lives. Just under half of the labour force (47 per cent) is now female. They are likely to have been divorced, separated or never married, and to have had more than one partner. They are likely to live alone – one-quarter of all households is now a one-person household. They may have been quite entrepreneurial, forced by the changes in the labour market to have held a succession of part-time or short-term jobs, or they may have been self-employed. An increasing number will have held senior managerial positions.

They will be more realistic and unsentimental. Many will have had to balance heavy caring responsibilities with careers, and they will know the true cost of caring. They are likely to have shared childcare with professional childminders, and will have had little time for active involvement in charities. Many will be pensioners.

These women will be computer and financially literate, having had to take more personal responsibility for taxes, mortgages, pensions and insurance, and having been targeted for such products by increasingly tailor-made marketing. Fiscal incentives will be increasingly attractive to this group. Much of their wealth may be held in pensions and insurance, so new giving tax reliefs linked to insurance pay-outs could be the next step in the development of tax incentives for giving. They are likely to shop and donate on-line.

To sum up, this potential high-net-worth pool of older women donors will be increasingly discriminating in its choice of charities, expecting evidence of success, particularly in areas such as vulnerable children. They may well choose causes that bear a direct relationship to the challenges faced in their own lives – cancer research and care (lung cancer, particularly, because of the rising rates of smoking among young women, and breast cancer because of its prevalence among middle-class, middle-aged women in the South), heart disease (an increasing threat to women as they adopt more 'male' lifestyles), carer support (with which they can identify), environmental issues (because of concerns about their children's future), and elderly people (as an increasing population group, which they will soon join). Their caring instincts, coupled with their power as consumers, could make them a key donor group.

Young philanthropist, London/South East, male (maybe not), must be successful wealthy entrepreneur

Do today's successful entrepreneurs contain the embryo of a new age of philanthropy? Faster growth in the creation of new trusts in particular seems a real possibility since the donor tax benefits for gifts of shares and securities were introduced. The market scope is considerable, as much of the new personal wealth is in the form of shares and securities, and the percentage of households with such assets has almost trebled over the last two decades to 23 per cent. Real household disposable income per head nearly doubled between 1971 and 1997, but ultimately the wealth of this group will be strongly linked to global markets.

Globalisation means that this group is ethnically diverse, international in origin and interests. Much more research needs to be carried out into this potential donor group, as very little is known about motivations or concerns. In the USA, they have been dubbed Bobos (bourgeois bohemians), young successful corporate entrepreneurs who combine a drive for market success with social concern and an interest in alternative lifestyles. US fundraisers are trying to capture their love of success and individual and corporate enterprise through promoting venture philanthropy to them. Such fundraising is likely to require a long-term investment from charities. Can the City's financial investors become the social investors of the future? John Kingston provides further thoughts on venture philanthropy in Chapter 9.

Corporate partner, view to long-term relationship, SSCSR (strong sense of corporate social responsibility), interested in CRM (cause-related marketing), chairperson actively involved in charity

CAF research among senior business leaders shows that half believe the involvement of senior business people in charities is an important feature of corporate social responsibility, although for the majority personal reward is a very strong motive for involvement.

This research showed that chairpersons give more than 10 hours per month of their time to charities. Company giving represents about £50 million per annum. Charities are constantly tantalised by the imagined potential of corporate giving. The level of corporate cash giving, however, has, in fact, barely grown over a decade of increasing company profits (although it is claimed that gifts in kind have grown). It is surely startlingly clear now to charities that they will only realise the potential for corporate support if they develop new forms of working with companies, in partnerships for mutual benefit.

Corporate social responsibility (CSR) is now clearly on the public agenda. A new era in corporate–charity partnerships could be opened up if charities could find ways of working more closely and imaginatively with companies. The promotion of payroll giving at all levels of the company, so that maximum advantage is taken of the government's recent removal of the upper limit for tax benefit, could, for example, become a key strand of CSR policy. Alternatively, joint initiatives could go well beyond simple brand linking to the development of shared values about lifestyles and future environments.

Corporate partners could be demanding – in the words of one company chairman who commented in the CAF research:

> You must make sure that your charitable giving is effective: it's not just a case of shovelling the money out of the door and saying 'I've done a wonderful job'; you may not have done any good at all.

Wanted: young donors, idealistic, must have interest in giving time as well as money

Many charities have traditionally ignored this group, in favour of targeting older, wealthier donors. As noted in previous sections, this neglect is reflected in a long-term decline in involvement, which has been noted in volunteering as well as in giving. Charities can no longer wait for such donors to grow older and richer before recruiting them, as the evidence is clear that successive cohorts of young people are decreasingly likely to get involved in giving as they get older – there is therefore a long-term decline in the potential pool of donors.

A recent (2001) survey undertaken by CAF with leading ISP Poptel (see www.CAFonline.org/research), and supported by many of Britain's top charities, identified a distinctive group of charity internet supporters that defies some of the usual stereotypes. They are:

- younger (aged 25–34),
- lower to middle income (£10,000–£30,000 yearly),
- equally likely to be men or women,
- heavy internet users (almost 60 per cent used the internet every day last year, excluding e-mail).

This highly sophisticated group of charity internet supporters actively seek out information about charities and the best ways to give to them. They consult several sources of information when deciding which charities to donate to, including fundraising appeal letters, charity newsletters, the internet, e-mail, TV, radio and newspaper articles. These e-donors are more likely to make a considered donation by plastic, or by regular payment using direct debit or covenants than by spontaneous cash payments. One-quarter already have made at least one online donation since April 2000, and over two-thirds of the group said that they would be likely to make an online donation in future.

They are financially astute. Almost two-thirds (64 per cent) of them use tax-effective giving methods, thereby allowing the charity to reclaim basic-rate tax on the donation and enabling higher-rate tax-paying donors to reclaim the difference between basic- and higher-rate tax.

This relatively young online community of sophisticated internet-literate individuals may be an increasingly important group for fundraisers of the future – not because they are especially rich (although their income will be rising), but because they are actively seeking to give to charities efficiently, quickly and in a way that suits their e-working lifestyle.

Charities are increasingly worried about falling numbers of donors, especially among younger people. Only one in five households in their 20s donates, compared with one in three households in their 60s. An estimated 1 per cent of the British public currently give to charities online, but, with over 10,000 new users coming online every day in Britain, and with increasing numbers of young people in particular becoming more internet-literate, the potential for fundraising from this group appears limited only by fundraisers' imaginations. Charities could learn a lot about internet fundraising from the ways in which today's online community use the net, and from their attitudes towards charities' websites and fundraising initiatives.

The younger donor population is fragmented into many smaller populations. It is ethnically diverse, with about one in ten coming from a minority ethnic background. It is multicultural and, with access to a huge range of media, can speedily develop subcultures. This has the advantage that the media can be used to promote charity causes and ways of giving in an immediate and lively way. Younger donors tend to support animal, environmental and international causes: charities will increasingly need to link into their subcultures. While a small proportion will be eagerly sought after in the shrinking high-tech labour market of the future, many face difficult futures, unemployment and welfare constraints. Many will be single parents. To capture the sympathies of this group, charities will need to be sensitive to diverse lifestyles, opportunities and values. Evidence from the British Social

Attitudes Surveys has shown that young donors are less cynical, but they need to know that their limited resources will not be wasted by charities and that the causes are appropriate. They tend to regard matters such as homelessness and British children in need as a government and not a charity responsibility. They need to believe that the cause is worthwhile, and they are much more likely to be motivated by the cause than the charity brand.

Charitable giving as a lifestyle

These donor profiles rehearse the key individual donor issues facing charities in the next few decades. The future population of donors will be diverse, and knowledgeable, with access to a huge range of information at the flick of a button. As consumers of charities' services they will be as demanding as they are of any other private goods and services in an economy in which the consumer is king. They may well become more demanding of charities as they look to the voluntary sector and the social economy more generally to redress the extremes of global capitalism.

References

Banks J and Tanner S (1997) *The State of Donation*. London: IFS.

Burnett K (1992) *Relationship Fundraising*. London: White Lion Press.

Future Foundation (2001) *Charity Awareness Monitor*, January 2001.

Jones R (2001) *The Big Idea*. London: HarperCollins.

NCVO (1998) 'Blurred Vision – public trust in charities'. *NCVO Research Quarterly*, **1**, January.

Lee S and Sargeant A (2001) 'Improving Public Trust in the Voluntary Sector: an empirical analysis.' (Henley Working Paper 0122). Henley on Thames: Henley Management College.

Passey A, Hems L and Jas P (2000) *The UK Voluntary Sector Almanac 2000*. London: NCVO.

Seligman A (1997) *The Problem of Trust*. Princeton NJ: Princeton University Press.

Tonkiss F and Passey A (1999) 'Trust, Confidence and Voluntary Organisations: between values and institutions.' *Sociology* **33**(2), 257–74.

7

ALTRUISM, GUILT AND THE FEEL-GOOD FACTOR – WHY DO PEOPLE GIVE TO CHARITY?

Catherine Walker

ALTRUISM – GENEROUS BY NATURE OR NURTURE?

If you have ever given to charity, ask yourself this question. Why did you do it?

It is not as simple a question as it sounds; nor is it easy to answer.

Charitable fundraisers would love to discover a magic formula for getting people to give. They are not alone: the philanthropic motive, the desire to give to others in society, has fascinated and puzzled philosophers and economists throughout history. More recently, despite receiving astonishingly little attention in the traditional social sciences, a growing amount of data from surveys of individual giving behaviour has prompted renewed interest, particularly from newer disciplines such as economic psychology, behavioural economics and economic sociology. The aim of this chapter is to review what we know about why people give and to explore some of the new evidence and theories emerging in these fields.

Giving is often associated with altruism, which is defined as a regard for others before oneself. As such, it is immediately in conflict with the predominant Darwinian theory of over-riding self-interest and the survival of the fittest by natural selection. Neo-Darwinian theory, such as Dawkins' idea of the selfish gene (1976), allows for altruism to occur if it benefits the individual's wider gene pool. Indeed, the 'gene question' is one that researchers into giving come up against relatively frequently. Is there an altruistic gene? Is it in people's nature to be generous or selfish? Is there a button marked 'altruism' that comes with some models and not others?

In strict neo-Darwinian terms, if pure altruism (ie beyond the wider gene pool posited by Dawkins) were genetically transmitted, it would eventually simply die out. But altruism (directed at anyone, not just kin) is alive and well in our society, so to explain its existence scientists have hypothesised that altruism might be maintained through cultural traditions, and that it might be ingrained in society through the continual advocacy of social institutions. Seen in this way, the act of giving money to charity could be viewed as a way of building up social trust and stability and contributing to a civil society.

THE ECONOMIC THEORY OF GENEROSITY

Neo-classical micro-economic theory, which dominates thinking about all financial interactions, is founded on the axiom of selfish rationality. In other words, people generally behave in a self-interested manner. Rational man as portrayed in neo-classical micro-economic theories – 'homo economicus' (Smith, 1908 (1776)) – would not give to charity, because there is no obvious personal economic gain. Given that charitable donations do take place, however, can economic theory accommodate giving to charity?

Some economists have proposed solutions to this problem by treating charitable giving not as a one-sided gift but as an exchange in which the donor receives some reciprocal benefit. These theories can be encapsulated in three broad schools of thought (Andreoni, 2001):

- The **public good theory** (the most popular theory) views charitable giving as funding a public good (like street lighting or the police). People give because society as a whole (including the giver) benefits from the provision of these services. The argument commonly raised against the public good theory is that people will free-ride (eg they will literally hop on the bus without paying the fare) and not contribute to public goods that are provided by others' contributions. In time, nobody would contribute. But, again, this is clearly not the case in reality. One counter-argument is to suggest that individuals hold moral principles that drive them to contribute their fair share as long as other people are contributing. There is some evidence to support these claims, but the support is patchy.

- The **exchange theory** of charitable giving proposes that individuals receive tangible rewards in return for their gifts: they may, for example, become members of an exclusive club of donors with special privileges, or their name may be engraved on a plaque in the local theatre they supported, or listed in the programme. Giving in this scenario acts as a signal of the individual's status in the community. Yet, while this may be a motivation for some gifts, the vast majority of gifts still go unrewarded in any tangible way.

- The '**warm-glow effect**' posits the idea of psychological benefits from giving. People feel good when they give to charity, and the more they give the better they feel. Many modern economists now accommodate the warm-glow effect as a core economic motivation for giving, but theories still fall short of understanding why, and are still unable to quantify the effect or to explain whether this is a stable trait that affects all people equally or some more than others.

Economic theory can be adapted to accommodate some of the intricacies of charitable giving, yet such models have remained largely untested – partly because of economists' lack of interest in motivations and partly because of the lack of appropriate data. It is not an easy task to find evidence that donors think about the longer-term or indirect benefit they may receive from the effects of their donation, or make the complicated mental calculations necessary to figure out their due proportional or 'fair' contribution in line with the rest of society.

So, while economic theories can provide partial explanations for giving to charity, they are short on proof and lacking in detail. Economists tend to regard individual preferences as given. Other approaches are needed to explore the fuller picture of why people give, and researchers in other disciplines have begun to look at how and why individual preferences for giving are distributed across the population.

WHAT INFLUENCES PEOPLE TO GIVE?

In Figure 7.1, a 'model' or picture of all the different influences that might bear on a decision to give is presented. It is based on theories and research from a wide range of approaches. These will be examined in the rest of this chapter, as each part of the model is examined in more detail to explore what each contributes to our understanding of why people give.

Figure 7.1   A figurative model of giving influences[1]

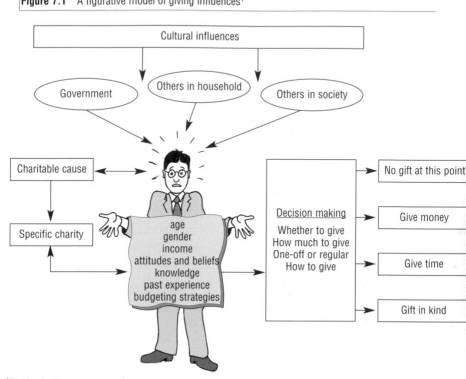

[1] The basic design of this schema owes much to Adrian Sargeant's 1999 marketing model of individual giving, which is presented in Chapter 8.

All in a good cause?

It might seem a natural and easy question to ask people 'Why do you give to charity?', but the fact is that most people do not give, generically, to 'charity'.[1] Most people give to a 'cause' or 'a named charity or charities'. The NCVO/NOP surveys have found that the general public attach very high levels of importance (89 per cent) to the kind of cause they are being asked to support when making their decision whether or not to give (CAF/IR/NCVO July 2000). But how

---

[1]   In this section, we are talking about giving to recognised charities rather than, for example, to people begging on the streets – although many of the other factors in the model would also influence other forms of giving.

do they make that all-important choice between competing causes and charities? In an increasingly competitive fundraising environment, how do people choose?

People tend to make judgements based on the information available to them, predominantly from the media, their educational background, friends, family and others, evaluating this information against previous experience and existing knowledge (Fenton et al, 1999). In the case of charities, people are often presented with partial information that does not enable them to make a thorough evaluation of either the cause or the specific charity. Unlike with some purchased goods or services, it is usually impossible for the donor to observe or evaluate the quality of the charity's work, because charities act as intermediaries in the process of putting the individual's donation to good use. People often make judgements based on partial information and on 'urban myths' about the effects of size and professionalism on a charity's efficiency and efficacy (see Table 7.1).[2]

Figures from the NCVO/NOP surveys have consistently shown that the public, when deciding whether or not to give, attaches high levels of importance to how much they trust the charity (84 per cent – CAF/IR/NCVO July 2000) and whether the charity can tell them how much of the money will reach the needy cause (66 per cent – CAF/IR/NCVO July 2000) (see Table 7.2). Despite better charity accounting standards, and the increasing availability of information (eg on the internet), it is difficult for the public to get hold of these kinds of fact. The effect of this is to force people into using less reliable sources of information to make their choices.

This is not to say that people make completely random or biased choices between charities. Where information is partial, however, a leap of faith, and a large degree of trust, is often necessary. Since trust has been alleged by some to be a prerequisite for giving to charities (Fenton et al, 1995), it is vital that the public has faith in

---

[2] *The tables of attitude statements in this chapter are taken largely from the British Social Attitudes Surveys from 1991 to 1996, except where stated. Although the vast majority of the surveys are based on a representative sample of adults in the UK, caution should be exercised when comparing different surveys from different years, as methodologies and contents differ.*

Table 7.1   Some beliefs held by the general population about charities (%)

Statement	Proportion agreeing (%)
There are so many charities that it is difficult to decide which one to give to.[1]	74
There's no point in giving money to the bigger charities because so little gets to the cause.[2]	49
The bigger the charity becomes, the more out of touch it gets with those it is trying to help.[1]	44
The smaller a charity, the more likely it is to put its money to good use.[1]	34
Nowadays charities can only do their job properly if they are run by paid professionals, not volunteers.[1]	21

[1]BSA (1991, 1996).
[2]Saxon-Harrold et al (1987).

charities. Andrew Passey discusses the issues of trust and confidence in charities in Chapter 6 of this book; here it is necessary only to note the importance of this factor in the debate over the causes of falling levels of giving to charity.

Table 7.2 shows how important issues of charities' accountability are to the public.

The effect of fundraising method on donors' attitudes

Turning from people's reasons for giving to their actual behaviour when making a gift, it is the exception rather than the rule that donors actively seek out a cause or charity to support. Work based on the Individual Giving Survey (IGS) covering monthly donations from 1990 to 1993 (Halfpenny et al, 1992, 1993, 1994) found that almost three-quarters of the population (74 per cent) had been approached at least once to make a donation, and that over 90 per cent of these actually gave at least once. In fact, fewer than 2 per cent of the

Table 7.2 Attitudes towards charities' accountability and issues of trust (%)

Statement	Proportion agreeing (%)
I like to know how much of my donations go on administration costs.[1]	73
Too often charities don't bother to say how the money they get is being spent.[2]	69
Charities waste too much money on administration.[3]	68
I like to support projects where you can see what your money has bought.[4]	55
Most charities are wasteful of their funds.[5]	34

[1]NCVO (1998).
[2]BSA (1991, 1993).
[3]MORI (1991).
[4]Saxon-Harrold et al (1987).
[5]BSA (1991).

population who were not approached by a charity gave unsolicited donations during the same period (Foster et al, 2000).

The impact of different types of fundraising approach will be dealt with in more detail by Adrian Sargeant in the next chapter; here it is important to note the size of the effect of the fundraising effort on the individual, something that is often overlooked in economic models of charitable giving. Besides prompting an actual gift, fundraising approaches reduce the need for donors to find out information themselves when choosing between charities or causes. They also, by providing a suitable mechanism for giving (an enclosed envelope or form to fill in), reduce any effort involved in the process. By reducing the 'costs' of giving in these ways, it has been argued that fundraising approaches enhance the net warm-glow effect for donors (Foster et al, 2000).

On the other side of the coin, more-direct fundraising methods (eg face-to-face) have been criticised by donors as using a form of 'emotional blackmail' to elicit gifts (see Table 7.3). Gifts given out of feelings of guilt, shame or embarrassment might be seen as providing relief from social or personal psychological discomfort, and not as motivated by any altruistic feeling at all. Professional and lay opinion is split as to the efficacy of such direct forms of fundraising, and probably the best answer is that they will work for some people and not others. The question of their morality is a different matter altogether.

For some, face-to-face encounters in a public place, witnessed by others, provide tangible benefits of increased social prestige, as well as psychological 'warm-glow' benefits. For others, the 'bystander' effect (Darley & Latané, 1968), where others are present and not giving, may inhibit their giving. Either way, the after-effect is as important as the feelings at the point of donation: donors who feel that they were coerced into giving in such encounters might end up feeling antagonistic towards the charity in question and disinclined to make further donations to this particular cause. Others may overcome their negative feelings and subsequently experience a warm glow. What is certain is that the context in which giving takes place can be crucial to the outcome.

Table 7.3 Some reactions of the general public to direct fundraising methods (%)

Statement	Proportion agreeing (%)
I can't refuse when someone comes to the door or approaches me in the street with a collecting tin.[1]	57
I can't refuse when someone comes to the door with a collecting tin.[2]	46
I often give because I feel too embarrassed to say 'No' when someone asks.[3]	25

[1]Saxon-Harrold et al (1987).
[2]BSA (1996).
[3]Foster et al (2000).

Individual attributes

Arguably the greatest influence on any individual's behaviour is their psychological make-up and personality. This will mediate all other influences. Very few of these attributes are believed to be 'givens', and many have their roots in childhood (the heavy influence of parents and early learning experiences of charity). Indeed, it has been argued that all behaviour is the result of social learning and conditioning, and that it is not subject to the kinds of cognitive processes implied in the model presented in Figure 7.1.

Demographic variables (age, gender and income) Giving generally increases with age, social class and income (although lower-income households have been shown to be proportionally more generous in their giving than higher-income households). There are also several notable gender differences: more women give than men, and women tend to give to more charities than men. Socio-demographic factors such as income, marital status and age affect the influence of other external factors. For example, marriage, income and, to a certain extent, age influence the number of social ties people have and the subsequent number of approaches by charitable organisations to donate (Hall and Febrarro, 1998).

Attitudes Recent work has suggested that differences between individuals in the decision to donate are largely a function of attitude (Sargeant, 1999). Certainly a great deal of attention has been paid to attitudes in empirical research on giving, and there is a large amount of attitudinal data on why people think that they give to charities (see Table 7.4). There is some evidence that attitudes coincide with demographics, so types and groups of giver can be identified on this basis – but this is far from the whole picture (as the model presented in Figure 7.1 illustrates). It should also be borne in mind that in research it is not always possible to differentiate between attitudes that pre-date the giving event, and might be causal, and those that occur after giving, and therefore represent some post-hoc justification.

Beliefs Many studies have shown that people professing a religious faith are significantly more likely to give to charity, but there is also research to suggest an influence on giving of belief systems that are not attached to particular faiths (eg Hall and Febrarro, 1998). This

Table 7.4   What people say about why they give to charity (%)

Statement	Proportion agreeing (%)
It's rewarding to feel you've helped people in some way.[1]	84
I give to charities because I want to support the good causes for which they work.[2]	>80
I help concerns where my family or friends are involved, eg school or scouts for my children.[1]	76
Personal circumstances make me give, like I had a friend who died of cancer, so I give to cancer charities.[1]	70
I give to charities because they help to create a better society for everybody by reducing the level of social problems.[2]	>60
I give to charities because I or my family may personally benefit from them at some stage.[2]	40
I give to charities because I like the feeling of being generous.[2]	>20

[1]Saxon-Harrold et al, 1987.
[2]Foster et al, 2000.

research reveals the heavy influences of childhood and cultural background, but suggests that each individual's belief system is ultimately unique. In relation to giving, psychological disciplines have tended to focus on such aspects as *empathy* (identifying mentally with someone), *sympathy* (sharing the same feelings as someone) and a belief in a 'just world'. For example, research has shown that giving increases when the recipient is perceived to be similar and familiar to the empathetic donor (eg Ray, 1998; Warren and Walker, 1991); sympathy with recipients has been shown to be mediated by how much people believe that they deserve to be helped; and people who believe in a just world where people generally 'get what they deserve' are less likely to give. It has also been suggested that the decisions of whether and how much to give will in part be influenced by people's knowledge or beliefs about the consequences of their donation and by the extent to which it meets internal psychological needs (eg Radley and Kennedy, 1995). For example, the need for recognition should result in a larger, more ostentatious donation.

Knowledge Chapter 5 showed how important knowledge and understanding are to the effective use of tax incentives. Knowledge about charities and their effectiveness in carrying out their missions is generally poor among the public, but can be crucial in determining giving choices. General social knowledge may also be important in recognising and understanding community and societal needs and how charitable contributions affect these (Hall and Febrarro, 1998). Another type of knowledge that has been shown to have a strong effect on giving is the personal experience or knowledge of people affected by the particular problems targeted by charities (eg having friends or family suffering from cancer). This has been shown to have an important personal emotional influence on deciding to give (see Table 7.4).

Past experience It has been shown (eg Mount, 1996) that an individual's past behaviour affects their giving. Research has shown regular giving to be very much a matter of habit – if you have given to X charity before, you are much more likely to give to it again, as long as it continues to meet your expectations. Habit makes it much easier to give, as the donor does not have to go through any complicated information search or an evaluation of new charities. The nature of a donor's past experience with a particular charity or charities will also affect their future giving behaviour. As discussed earlier, donors who feel coerced into giving may be less inclined to give in future, whereas, if a charity has made them feel good about giving, this will increase the chances of a recurrent gift. Adrian Sargeant expands on this in the following chapter.

Budgeting strategies Economic psychology has drawn attention to budgeting strategies (or mental accounting) – the theory that people do not treat all money as the same, and budget for things in individual ways. They may hold a number of different mental (and sometimes physical) accounts for different types of income and expenditure. People often, for example, treat unexpected or irregular income (such as a bonus at work or a small win on the National

Lottery) differently from their regular income and spend it on more 'frivolous' things such as holidays and luxury items. From which source of income do people give to charity? Do they have separate 'funds of sympathy' (Young and Burgoyne, unpub) for different groups of cause, or is there one generic mental purse/pot for all charities? How is this budgeted alongside other competing consumption? Is giving seen as a necessity or a luxury good? Bound up in this are donors' perceptions of their ability to give, which has been shown to affect their decisions in this area. A person who is concerned about their financial stability may be less likely to give. Research has suggested that it is a person's perceived financial well-being which is important here, not the reality. Some recent work has suggested, for example, that Britons perceive themselves to be less well-off than comparable individuals in the USA and has offered this as a partial explanation for the differences in giving levels between the two countries (Wright, 2001).

The influence of others in the household

Most economic models assume that the individual makes decisions to give, or not to give, in isolation, without reference to other people in their household (their partner, a member of their family, or an unrelated other) or their social groups. Contrary to this, more-recent work in economic sociology, social psychology and other such disciplines has suggested that giving, like other decisions, often takes account of others' wishes, desires, hopes and feelings, either consciously or subconsciously.

One question that has plagued survey work on giving is the matter of whether giving is a personal or a household decision.[3] In fact, CAF CAF/IR/NCVO 2001 have shown that around 40 per cent of people who live with a partner discuss their decisions to give to charity with them sometimes (29 per cent) or often (12 per cent). People also discuss decisions with their parents (33 per cent of those living with them: mainly young people), their children (24 per cent of those

---

[3] *Giving surveys are split between those that ask about household giving (eg the Family Expenditure Survey), those that ask about personal giving (eg the Individual Giving Survey, and NCVO/NOP surveys), and those that use personal or household income as an indicator of relative wealth in this regard (see Chapter 3 for the differences between surveys).*

Table 7.5 How often donors discuss whether to give to charity with anyone else in their household[1] (%)

	Never	Sometimes	Often	Very often
Spouse or partner	59	29	6	6
Parent(s)	67	28	5	–
Child(ren)	76	18	5	1
Other relative(s)	81	14	3	2
Other unrelated person(s)	80	20	–	–

Source CAF questions in NCVO/NOP 2001.

[1]Sample = representative GB adults (over 16 years); base = all adults living in same household as named other; people could answer as many categories as applied.

living with them), other relatives (19 per cent) and other unrelated people in the household (20 per cent). The numbers were slightly lower for discussing *how much* to give but followed roughly the same trends (see Tables 7.5 and 7.6).

The most common reason for discussing a decision to give to charity was when considering how much the individual or household could afford to give. This is likely to be linked to whether giving is perceived to be a necessity or a luxury for that particular household or individual, and this in turn linked to many other factors (of which one of the most significant will be income). It is interesting to note that, while 61 per cent of people claimed that the money they gave to charity was totally their own money, 27 per cent said that some, most, or all of it was their partner's money, and 24 per cent said that some, most, or all of it was joint money. This further underlines the need to understand the complex relationships involved in decisions to give to charity – and fundraisers should not assume that all decisions are down to just one independent individual.

Table 7.6 How often donors discuss how much to give to charity with anyone else in their household (%)

	Never	Sometimes	Often	Very often
Spouse or partner	67	21	6	6
Parent(s)	73	23	4	–
Child(ren)	82	14	3	1
Other relative(s)	93	3	3	1
Other unrelated person(s)	8	15	–	–

Source CAF questions in NCVO/NOP 2001.

The influence of the government

The way the individual perceives the government's role in society (and the way the government perceives its own role) can be crucial to a person's attitude towards charitable giving. Little recent research is available on this, but earlier data indicate that if an individual believes that it is the government's responsibility to fund provision of certain services, then they may be less willing to support charitable provision of these services (see Table 7.7).

This relationship is not always clear cut. As Table 7.7 shows, the majority of people feel that the government has a responsibility to fund good works, yet many of them also give to charity themselves. This creates an uneasy and complicated relationship between government funding and people's donations. In repeated British Social Attitudes surveys (BSA 1991, 1993), around 65 per cent of the population feel that the more money people give to British charities the less the government will spend on people in need and that giving to charities somehow 'lets the government off the hook'. Beliefs about who should fund the provision of charitable services differ according to the kind of cause. Table 7.8 shows that helping British people came out as the perceived priority for the government's

Table 7.7 The general public's attitudes towards the role of the government in charity

Statement	Proportion agreeing (%)
The government has a basic responsibility to take care of people who can't take care of themselves.[1]	91
The government ought to help more, not rely on charities to raise needed money.[1]	87
The government should do less for the needy and encourage charities to do more.[2]	8

[1]Halfpenny et al (1993).
[2]BSA (1991, 1993).

responsibility. Charities were seen to be much more responsible for animals and overseas causes, although the government was seen to have a responsibility to share the financial burden here. This allocation of varying responsibility is also borne out by giving statistics which show that international aid is one of the most popular charitable causes in Britain (and is far higher up the list than in other countries – Salamon and Anheier, 1994.).

There are four main ways in which the government and their policies may affect individual giving to charities. In economic terms, these are 'crowding out', the 'demonstration effect', the 'income effect' and the 'price or incentive effect'. Each of these is clarified and assessed below.

- **Crowding out** is said to happen when state funding of charitable provision is seen to be adequate enough to make it unnecessary for the public to donate, and private donations are crowded out. Conversely, economic theory dictates that 'crowding in' should mean greater public donations when government funding is seen as inadequate. However, there is little empirical evidence to

Table 7.8 The public's attitude to which causes government or charities should support (%)

Cause	Government (not charities) should support (1995) (%)	Responsibility should be shared (1995) (%)	Charities (not government) should support (1995) (%)
Housing for homeless people in Britain	78	14	3
Food aid for starving people in poor countries	18	36	37
Helping British children in need	65	27	5
Helping children in need throughout the world	18	41	35
Helping to prevent cruelty to animals in Britain	11	34	46
Helping/Holidays for disabled people in Britain	32 (1993)	32	32 (1993)

support either of these effects to any great degree. Of course, the effect of government funding depends on how people actually view it, as discussed above.

- **The demonstration effect**, conversely, is said to occur (eg Jones et al, 1998) when government support for the charitable sector is high, actually encouraging people to give. This is known as the 'demonstration effect'. There has been some limited evidence for this theory, showing that government grants to a charity may act as a signal of its worthiness, enhancing its reputation as respectable, trustworthy and genuine in the eyes of potential donors, and increasing donations. The demonstration effect theoretically reduces the cost of giving by providing a short cut to judging which charities are most worthy of donations without having to search out information on all the different possible charities in the area.

- **The income effect**, much vaunted by the present Conservative opposition, predicts greater giving due to greater income – brought about, for example, by lower income tax. Standard economic theory dictates that greater income generally leads to greater spending in all categories. This theory finds partial support in giving survey data which shows that higher-income households tend to give more in absolute terms, but this is countered by evidence that lower-income households tend to give a greater proportion of their income.

- **The incentive, or price, effect** of tax reliefs has already been discussed in Chapter 5; here it suffices to say that the theory is that tax reliefs provide an economic incentive by lowering the cost or price of giving, and a psychological incentive in the shape of added tax back to the charity.

It is immensely difficult to isolate any one effect from the others, especially where these interact. For example, the incentive effect of tax reliefs is lessened by a reduction in the marginal tax rate (since there is then less tax relief available), but this may be off-set by any income effect of the same tax cuts. All these different and sometimes competing effects made it peculiarly difficult to predict the effects of the introduction of the new tax changes in April 2000, as discussed in the previous chapter. Thus great care should be taken when trying to support or oppose certain government policies on the grounds of their effects on charitable donations.

The influence of society and social groups

Social norms have been found to influence specific factors such as the timing of a gift, its size and who the recipients will be. Social norms may operate in a wide sense as societal expectations of some giving (eg blood donation), or in a more narrow sense as part of the rules of a social group or institution. The social psychological theory of social identity – that people have several social identities according to the groups they belong to in society – might be useful in trying to understand how social norms affect charitable giving. Social norms may influence a person in different ways in different situations according to how strong their social ties are, for example, and whether they are with other members of their social groups when they make their giving decision. Giving can be a vehicle to group membership or acceptance, or it can serve to affirm and maintain a desired social identity (eg membership of the church, Rotary or Lions club). Membership of associations and groups has been shown to increase giving. Several studies have attempted to measure the strength, type and number of social ties an individual has in relation to their participation and giving behaviour. Some have found evidence of an independent effect of a person's social ties on their giving, even when the effects of the fundraising approach and any benefit from giving have been discounted. Charitable giving in this context is seen to create and strengthen social networks and social capital (Gainer, 2001).[4]

THE DECISION TO GIVE

Having made a decision to give (as a result of the various influences already discussed), the donor then has to decide how much to give, whether to make this a one-off or regular payment, and how to give. Giving to charity, as Chapters 5 and 6 have shown, comes in many guises. The majority of charitable giving in Britain is spontaneous 'spare change giving'; only a small proportion is planned and tax-effective giving; and some is 'purchase giving' (eg buying in charity shops). Little work has been done on how people choose between these different methods of giving and how that choice fits in with their motivations to give. The holistic 'model' proposed here suggests that all these considerations are part of the same decision-making process and subject to the same influences, although they may not take place at the same time or in quite the same way: for example, a donor wishing to make a small one-off donation may choose to give cash, while a donor wishing to make a large regular commitment may choose to volunteer for the organisation instead of making a gift of money at this point.

Gifts of time, of money or in kind There is little or no research that examines the choice between giving time, money or gifts in kind.

---

[4] *Social group membership has also been shown to improve life expectancy. Robert Putnam has estimated that joining a social group halves your chances of dying in the next 12 months!*

Generally research on volunteering and donating have, despite their similarities, been separate endeavours. They are closely linked, with nearly all individuals who give time also tending to give money – 96 per cent according to the National Survey of Volunteering (Davis Smith, 1997). Perhaps the biggest difference between giving and volunteering is in the proportions who get involved because they are asked (47 per cent for volunteering, 90 per cent for giving) as opposed to those who actively seek involvement (48 per cent for volunteering, 2 per cent for giving) (Davis Smith, 1997; Foster et al, 2000). So giving is seen as much more responsive, and volunteering as perhaps more motivated. Around one-half of adults in Britain volunteer, with just under one-third (30 per cent) making a regular monthly commitment. The profile of volunteers as compared with givers shows similar patterns of demographics – it is not just those with 'time on their hands' who give time; in fact, those most likely to volunteer are those with substantial other calls on their time (Davis Smith, 1997).

A survey of British business leaders carried out by CAF and Deloitte & Touche in 2000 suggested that over two-thirds (70 per cent) of senior managers in Britain's top companies give some time to charities, voluntary or community organisations.[5] This extremely busy group of individuals claimed that their motivations for giving time and not just money were largely personal, with some corporate concerns also evident (see Table 7.9). In general, individuals giving time by volunteering tend to cite the enjoyment of helping, the satisfaction of seeing results, meeting people and making new friends and the sense of personal achievement as motivations for their involvement (Davis Smith, 1997). So while time may be more difficult to give than money, it seems that the rewards may be greater as well.

Gifts in kind are an increasingly popular way of companies giving to charities. From donating old computers to matching staff time for volunteering, corporate gifts are a growing market. There is little or no research into how and why companies decide to donate gifts of

[5] Making Time for Charity *(Walker and Pharoah, 2000) surveyed 111 companies in the FTSE350 list, with responses from mainly the chairman, chief executive, finance director, marketing and human resources directors.*

Table 7.9 British business leaders' personal motivations for being involved with charities

Motivation for giving time	Proportion of responses mentioning this motivation (%)
Giving something back to the community	33
Personal identification with a cause	13
A sense of corporate responsibility	10
Belief in worthy causes	4
A useful outlet for individual skills	4
Asked to be involved	3
The job needs doing	2
Involvement of others	2

stock or facilities instead of or as well as time and money. Different companies place different emphases on gifts in kind. For many it will be a financial decision, although primarily motivated by concerns of doing good. One study of small companies found that their charitable giving was principally reactive, responding to requests for help, rather than planned – much like individual giving (Halfpenny et al, 1998). More research in this area could help us to understand the full range of gifts to charity and the importance of including all forms of giving when measuring companies' support for charities. The establishment of such organisations as Gifts in Kind (UK) will contribute to the understanding and facilitation of in-kind giving. Individuals may also support charities in kind, for example by donating goods to charity shops, and this too should be included in models and measurement of giving.

CULTURAL CONSIDERATIONS: A BRITISH CULTURE OF GIVING?

Cultural influences overarch the entire picture we are presenting of the giving decision process (see Figure 7.1). In the increasingly global society we live in, these cultural influences are no longer narrowly defined. Certainly the media we are exposed to, particularly the TV and the internet, are not nationally defined, although many of the newspapers we read have heavy cultural biases. Studies suggest that national boundaries are still relatively strong in determining at least some of the factors that influence a person's giving decisions. The British are somewhat unique in their patterns of giving when compared with many other countries: participation rates are relatively high, but the amounts given are low (Salamon and Anheier, 1994).

In a recent *Guardian* opinion poll the general public voted overwhelmingly in agreement with the question 'Are the British public becoming more selfish than they used to be?' (82 per cent said 'Yes'). This vote took place on the same day as an annual conference organised by the Economic and Social Research Council, which debated whether Britain was becoming a nation of individuals rather than a community. The *Guardian* opinion poll also found that an overwhelming majority of the British public agreed when asked 'Are governments failing to act on the collective concerns of individuals?' (82 per cent said 'Yes'). Given that there has already been evidence of broad support for the government's taking a larger role in charitable funding, this comes as no surprise; however, we have also seen that people are willing to fund charities themselves.

A recent study (CAF/IR/NCVO 2000) found that the British culture of giving to charities is generous, motivated and responsible (see Table 7.10). The results of this survey also suggested answers to some of the questions posed by some of the economic and other theories of giving discussed earlier in this chapter.

This survey found that two-thirds (67 per cent) of the British population believe that they have a personal responsibility to give to charities and not just leave it up to others to contribute. Similarly, two-thirds (69 per cent) of people said that they were not influenced by how much other people gave, preferring instead to make their own decisions. This suggests that most people do not free-ride on the contributions of others, but feel motivated to give themselves.

Table 7.10 British attitudes towards giving to charity[1]

Statement	Proportion agreeing (%)	Proportion disagreeing (%)
I prefer to give money to charities that do not get enough financial support from the government.	54	17
There is no point in giving money to charities that are strongly supported by the government.	27	44
It does not really matter whether I give to charity or not, as other people will give anyway.	11	67
I only get pleasure from seeing the work done by charity if I have made a donation myself.	20	59
I prefer to give money to charity in a way that will allow the charity to claim an additional sum from the taxman.	46	20
I prefer to give money to charity in a way that will allow me to reduce my tax bill.	14	52
I feel that I should give as much money to charity as other people I know.	10	69

[1]This table shows questions from CAF/IR/NCVO 2000.

The CAF questions in CAF/IR/NCVO 2000 also found that 54 per cent of people preferred to support causes that do not get enough financial support from the government. This suggests that 'crowding in' is occurring for many people – stepping in to make up for a lack of government funding. Yet 44 per cent say that they would support causes that are strongly supported by the government, suggesting some evidence for the 'demonstration effect' as well. Almost half (46 per cent) felt it is important for them to be able to direct extra government money to their favourite causes through tax-effective giving, while only 14 per cent said they would use tax reliefs for their own gain. This may reflect social desirability, or the low proportion of higher-rate tax payers in the population, but it shows the apparent appeal of the principle of tax incentives, even if take-up is still restricted (see Chapter 5 for a more detailed discussion of tax incentives).

Charities should not become complacent, however, since it is evident from many studies that something of a cultural sea-change is occurring (not only in Britain but also globally). Modern standards of financial accountability and a growing awareness of the need for large multi-national companies to take greater social responsibility will affect attitudes to charities too.

Phenomena such as ethical consumption (buying fairly traded products and ethically sourced goods) and ethical investment, once thought the exclusive behaviour of a small minority of 'cranks', are on the increase. A report by the National Consumer Council in 1996 found that ethical consumers could most easily be distinguished from other consumers by their belief that 'they can make a difference'. Similarly, psychologists investigating ethical investors found that a prime motivation is the feeling that they are 'filling the gap of moral responsibility left by uncaring governments' (Lewis and Mackenzie, 1997). These expressions are remarkably similar to the motivations evinced by those giving to charity and should not be ignored by the public, private or charitable sectors.

The National Lottery

It might be argued that the National Lottery has become a key part of Britain's social and financial culture since its debut in 1994. The British Social Attitudes (BSA) survey in 1997 found three-quarters of the population had played the Lottery. There have also been several theories about its effect on charitable donations. For example, it has been asserted that the majority of people view the National Lottery as a charitable institution (Passey and Hems, 1997). The BSA found that 40 per cent of people thought that a 'great deal' or 'quite a lot' of money goes from the Lottery to 'charities and other good causes', while in fact only 28 pence in every £1 goes to 'good causes'.

In 1997, the British public seemed split over whether playing the Lottery affects the amount of money people in general give to 'good causes' in other ways. They were more certain when it came to themselves: 91 per cent said it did not affect the amount they personally gave to 'good causes' in other ways. Like the British public, researchers are also split in their opinion about the effect of the Lottery on charitable donations.

CONCLUSIONS

A more comprehensive model of giving influences such as the one presented here has not yet been empirically tested: to do so would present no easy task.[6] Asking people why they give often meets with a wall of mis-remembering, imputed justifications after the event, and answers heavily influenced by social desirability.

There is enough research related to motivations to give, or 'altruism', to indicate that it is a very complex matter. Reasons why people give to charity are complicated, diverse, and sometimes contradictory, and are determined by a wide variety of social relationships, beliefs and circumstances. They can vary between individuals as well as between groups of individuals, and they can change with a person's circumstances and/or beliefs, and even vary when a person is presented with different giving scenarios. The various different factors in this model all interact with each other in complex ways. The very diversity of the charitable sector itself reflects this complexity. Giving is part of an intricate economic, social and psychological system of exchanges which characterises people's everyday lives, and which involves a degree of both selfishness and selflessness. Whether consciously or unconsciously, charities tap into this wide range of motivations and needs.

The simple messages to emerge for charities are that they should provide more detailed information about efficiency, about the success of projects, about themselves as organisations. They should make this information much more widely available so that individuals can make an informed choice – especially where the charity is not a large well-established brand name that can rely both on habit and, to a certain extent, the goodwill of donors (although for how long?). The more complex message is that charitable support occurs within a public and social context that in itself will influence overall support for charitable behaviour. Influencing this wider context requires charities to engage with many stakeholders, from government to beneficiaries.

---

[6] *Some models worth looking at in this respect are Radley and Kennedy, 1995; Schervish and Havens, 1997; Hall and Febrarro, 1998; Sargeant, 1999.*

For fundraisers, several things should be borne in mind. It has been shown that the fundraising method materially affects the size of the gift; the amount asked for will have a strong influence on the donor, and some critics have pointed to the '£2 a month' approach as contributing to Britain's 'spare change mentality' (Wright, 2001) towards charity. It should also be noted that the number of times a person is approached within a given time significantly decreases the probability of their making a donation at all (Foster et al, 2000).

It is therefore of deep concern that it is not the whole of British society that is giving and participating in community and voluntary activity. The young have been seen to be dropping off the scale when it comes to giving; and those 'from lower socio-economic classes, the unemployed and those with lower educational achievements' (NCVO, 2000) are increasingly under-represented in terms of participation in formal social relationships.

Models such as the one presented here are only useful insofar as they relate directly to the situation of the individual charity or person in question. Charities have only a limited amount of information about donors, so a certain amount of scepticism is healthy. Of ultimate benefit to any charity fundraiser will be the ability to answer the question 'What makes people give to my specific charity, and what might I do to make more people give and give more?' This process will be examined in the next chapter, using a detailed marketing model of individual charity-giving behaviour with a focus on how charities can influence giving decisions.

Note

The author gratefully acknowledges comments on an earlier draft of this chapter by Professor Paul Webley, Social and Economic Psychology Research Group, University of Exeter, and Professor Peter Halfpenny, Centre for Applied Social Research, Department of Sociology, University of Manchester.

References

Andreoni J (2001) 'The Economics of Philanthropy' in Smelser N J & Baltes P B (eds) *International Encyclopedia of the Social and Behavioural Sciences*. London: Elsevier.

BSA (1991, 1993, 1996) British Social Attitudes Survey (unpublished reports). West Malling: CAF.

Darley J and M Latané B (1968) 'Bystander Intervention in Emergencies: diffusion of responsibility'. *Journal of Personality and Social Psychology*, **8**: 377–383.

Davis Smith J (1997) *The 1997 National Survey of Volunteering*. London: The National Centre for Volunteering.

Dawkins R (1976) *The Selfish Gene*. Oxford University Press.

Fenton N, Golding P and Radley A (1995) 'Charities, Media and Public Opinion'. *Research Bulletin*, Winter 1995, **37**: 10–15. London: HMSO.

Fenton N, Passey A and Hems L (1999) 'Trust, the Voluntary Sector and Civil Society'. *International Journal of Sociology and Social Policy*, **19**(7/8) 21–42.

Foster V, Mourato S, Pearce D and Ozdemiroglu E (2000) *The Price of Virtue: the economic value of the charitable sector*. Cheltenham: Edward Elgar.

Gainer B (2001) 'Social Capital and Philanthropy: the impact of social embeddedness on charitable giving' in ARNOVA Conference Abstracts 2001, proceedings of the 30th annual conference of the Association for Research on Nonprofit Organisations and Voluntary Action, 28 November–1 December, Miami, Florida, USA.

Halfpenny P, Hudson W and Jones J (1998) 'Small Companies' Charitable Giving'. *Working Papers in Applied Social Research*, No 23, Department of Sociology, University of Manchester.

Halfpenny P, Pettipher C and Saxon-Harrold S K E (1992) *Individual Giving and Volunteering in Britain: who gives what and why?* 5th edn. West Malling: CAF.

Halfpenny P, Pettipher C and Saxon-Harrold S K E (1993) *Individual Giving and Volunteering in Britain: who gives what and why?* 6th edn. West Malling: CAF.

Halfpenny P, Pettipher C and Saxon-Harrold S K E (1994) *Individual Giving and Volunteering in Britain: who gives what and why?* 7th edn. West Malling: CAF.

Hall M and Febrarro A (1998) 'Models of Charitable Giving: identification or planned donations?' Presentation at the 27th Annual Conference of ARNOVA, Seattle, Washington, 5–7 Nov, 1998.

Jones P, Cullis J, and Lewis A (1998) 'Public Versus Private Provision for Altruism'. *Kyklos* **51**: 3–24.

Lewis A and Mackenzie C (1997) 'Morals, Motives and Money: the case of UK ethical investing' in the proceedings of the XXII International Colloquium of Economic Psychology. Promolibro: Valencia, vol. 1, pp107–117.

MORI (1991, unpublished) 'Public attitudes to charities'. Research study conducted for CAF, December.

Mount J (1996) 'Why Donors Give'. *Nonprofit Management & Leadership*, **7**(1): 3–14.

NCVO (1998) 'Blurred Vision – public trust in charities'. *NCVO Research Quarterly*, **1**, January.

NCVO (2000) 'Coming Apart – or Coming Together? New findings on social participation and trust in Britain'. *NCVO Research Quarterley*, **11**.

Passey A and Hems L (1997) *Charitable giving in Great Britain*. London: NCVO.

Radley A and Kennedy M (1995) 'Charitable Giving by Individuals – a study of attitudes and practice'. *Human Relations*, **48**: 685–709.

Ray L (1998) 'Why We Give: testing economic and social psychological accounts of altruism'. *Polity*, **30**: 383–415.

Salamon L M and Anheier H K (1994) *The Emerging Sector: an overview*. Baltimore: The Johns Hopkins University Institute for Policy Studies.

Sargeant A (1999) 'Charity Giving: towards a model of donor behaviour'. *Journal of Marketing Management*, **15**: 215–238.

Saxon-Harrold S K E, Carter J and Humble S (1987) *The Charitable Behaviour of the British People: a national survey of patterns and attitudes to charitable giving*. West Malling: CAF.

Schervish P G, and Havens J J (1997) 'Social Participation and Charitable Giving: a multivariate analysis.' *Voluntas*, **8**(3): 235–260.

Smith A (1908) *An Enquiry into the Wealth and Causes of the Wealth of Nations*. London: Bell. (Originally published 1776).

Walker C and Pharoah C (2000) *Making Time for Charity: a survey of top UK business leaders' involvement with voluntary organisations*. West Malling: Kent.

Warren P E and Walker I (1991) 'Empathy, Effectiveness and Donations to Charity: social psychology's contribution'. *British Journal of Social Psychology,* **30**: 325–337.

Wright K (2001) 'Generosity vs. Altruism: philanthropy and charity in the US and UK'. *Voluntas* **12**(4).

Young B M and Burgoyne C B, 'Why Do People Give To Charity?' A review of the literature for CAF (unpublished report).

8

WHAT TURNS DONORS ON?
WHAT TURNS THEM OFF?
Adrian Sargeant

HOW FUNDRAISING TECHNIQUES INFLUENCE GIVING AND LOYALTY TO CHARITIES

In the previous chapter, Catherine Walker reviewed the many considerations and influences that may be jostling for position in the potential donor's mind when considering a gift. This chapter focuses on how charities and fundraisers attempt to influence these processes with their marketing and communications techniques. We will review what we know about giving, the individuals who give and the factors that drive them to increase their commitment. We will also examine what can go wrong in fundraising relationships and cause a donor to terminate their support. Throughout, the approach taken will be to provide an overview of the available research rather than to attempt to provide a comprehensive review of any one aspect of giving.

To provide a framework for our discussion we will group the available research using the headings depicted in the model in Figure 8.1. In the sections below we consider each aspect of the model in turn.

CONSIDERATIONS AND INFLUENCES IN DECISION ABOUT GIFTS

As Figure 8.1 clearly indicates, there are a number of external considerations and influences to the decision-making process of anyone who is going to make a gift. Charities currently engage in a variety of different fundraising appeals driven by an equally wide range of fundraising techniques. These have included direct mail, telemarketing, face-to-face canvassing, door-to-door distribution, press advertising and, increasingly, internet, radio advertising and DRTV. We know from research that the profile of supporter likely to respond to each of these media is slightly different and that the behaviour of each category subsequently is also somewhat different. DRTV donors, for example, tend to give gifts slightly above that which might be achieved through the use of direct mail, but they are notoriously difficult to engage with for a second and subsequent gift.

We also know that each medium will differ somewhat in terms of its performance for both donor-recruitment and donor-development activities. Most charities will lose money on recruitment, earning an average of only 75p per £1 of investment. This tends to vary by recruitment media employed (off-the-page advertising performing particularly poorly), size of the organisation and the category of cause for which one is raising funds. Cancer-related charities and children's charities tend to achieve slightly higher returns than those working in other parts of the sector. By contrast, when looking at development activity, charities typically achieve a return of around £5 for every £1

Figure 8.1 A model of individual charity giving behaviour

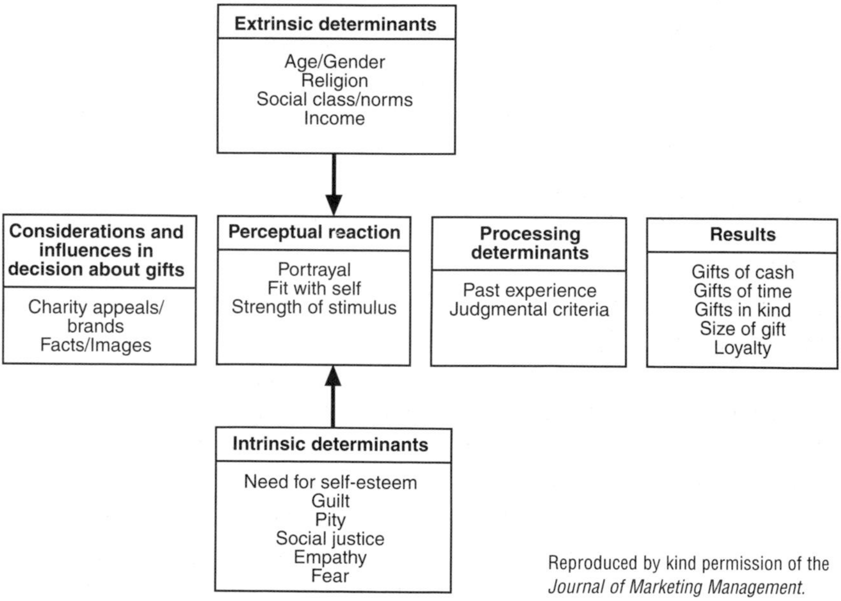

Reproduced by kind permission of the
Journal of Marketing Management.

of investment. It is clearly here where most organisations make their fundraising pay, although it should be noted that the same size and sector effects apply.

The power of branding

The point about size is particularly important. While there would appear to be economies of scale inherent to fundraising activity, many of the larger organisations also have well-known successful brands, which reduce the risk for potential donors in offering donations and limit the need to explain every aspect of what an organisation stands for in a fundraising message. Brands act as a simple hook on which donors may store and memorise information, and prospective donors build up such knowledge over time. In the voluntary sector, successful branding at an organisational level can lead to successful fundraising, with such success driven by the ability to use the brand to project the beliefs and values of the organisation's stakeholders. While these are perhaps rather less tangible than the facts about why an organisation exists and the nature of the beneficiary group, this latter class of variables can greatly aid a donor's understanding of the charity concerned and suggest very potent reasons why it might be worthy of support. It is only comparatively recently that there has been much formal interest in branding within the sector. However, while historically charities may have not described much of what they do as 'branding', organisations have long been concerned with maintaining a consistent style and tone of voice and conducting periodic reviews of both policies and actions to ensure that a consistent personality is projected. It has been argued that the clarity with which this 'personality' is projected will have a direct impact on an organisation's ability to fundraise.

Adopting the most successful approaches

It also seems clear that the approach adopted within each respective medium will affect the pattern of support exhibited. Much of what we now understand about this influence on behaviour is driven by research conducted by the plethora of agencies involved in the realm of direct marketing. The joy of this particular medium is that it is infinitely testable, making it possible to ascertain exactly the right approach for each client. In face-to-face recruitment, for example, we know the following:

- Lowering the sums requested tends to increase the agreement to give. Charities such as Oxfam have found considerable merit in asking for £2 per month, generating an adequate return on investment over the full duration of a supporter's relationship with the organisation.

- Legitimising paltry contributions can increase response – using phrases such as 'every penny will help' does actually increase compliance and can greatly improve the response in face-to-face forms of solicitation in particular.

- There is evidence of a 'foot-in-the-mouth' effect. Starting a request for support by asking people how they feel, acknowledging their response and *only then* asking for a donation greatly enhances compliance. The psychologists tell us that this is because people will behave in a manner consistent with how they have described themselves as feeling.

- The gender of the fundraiser has an impact: females generate more compliance than males.

- The degree to which the fundraiser appears 'similar' to the prospective giver increases compliance. People tend to give to people they perceive as similar to themselves.

- Where the request for support is made can also make a difference: locations such as exits/entrances to buildings hinder the prospective giver's escape and make it much more likely that they will give because they do not want to be seen by others as uncaring.

In direct mail, we know that the way the print looks, and how it links with illustrations and photographs, will have an effect on readers' response: certain fonts and font sizes work better than others; pictures generate more attention than text (or headlines); pictures of people work particularly well, as our attention is drawn to the eyes of the subject presented. We even know that pictures of groups of subjects work better than pictures of individuals alone.

In short, there is a wealth of knowledge available to guide the nature of the approach that should be taken in each medium if the maximum response is to be engendered.

HOW PEOPLE PERCEIVE AND REACT TO MESSAGES

Whatever form the request for support might eventually take, there are a variety of factors that are likely to influence a potential donor's perception of and reaction to the message being conveyed. Again, a wealth of research is available in this area, to which it is not possible to do full justice here. Donors receiving positively framed messages, designed to make them feel good, are statistically more likely to respond than donors offered primarily negative messages, designed to make them feel bad. Most significant, however, are the portrayal of the individual(s) in need, the fit of the charity with a given donor's self-image and the strength of the stimulus. Each of these will now be considered in turn.

How beneficiaries are portrayed

The manner in which recipients of the charitable 'product' are portrayed can have an impact on donors' ability to remember the message, their attitudes towards support and their actual giving behaviour. Donors will tend to support those charities that represent the needy in an acceptable way. Pictures, for example, of an overtly disabled child have been shown actually to decrease the response to door-to-door giving solicitations.

Appeals for charities concerned with disability often emphasise the dependability of those individuals with the respective disability. There is now considerable evidence that such appeals are very successful in engendering feelings of sympathy, guilt and pity. These are all emotions that are strongly correlated with enhanced levels of support.

For many such organisations, however, it is often very difficult to decide on the degree to which dependency should be depicted in fundraising communications. Research tells us that greater degrees of perceived dependency are related to greater degrees of help – at least in general. The real key here lies in understanding whether the dependency will be perceived as permanent or temporary. In the case of the former, the level of dependency has no effect on the amount likely to be given; in the case of the latter, higher levels of dependency can lead to greater willingness and higher levels of donation.

It is important to note that, while it may be effective in fundraising communications to depict the needy in a particular way, research also tells us that there are wider ramifications. Portraying recipients as succumbing to their condition can have a powerful impact on the subsequent attitudes of the donor. In the case of disabled people, the long-term interests of the beneficiary group can be harmed by reinforcing negative stereotypes and attitudes. Positive portrayals on the other hand seem to engender positive attitudes.

Research also tells us that attractive people are perceived as more worthy than unattractive people, and that female subjects would appear to engender greater rates of compliance than male subjects. The extent to which recipients might be seen as contributing to their own condition can also be a factor in behaviour. Those that are seen as being in some way responsible for their own condition attract less willingness to give and lower levels of support.

Fit with donor's desired self-image

We know that individuals are more likely to help those they perceive as being similar to themselves. They will thus tend to filter out those messages from charities that support segments of society they feel no connection with. Of course, charities exist to support work, not only with other people but also wider environmental or ecological concerns, from which everyone can ultimately stand to benefit. Giving to these causes can be explained by reference to one's self-image. Giving to certain organisations can enhance or aid self-worth, and these are factors that may obviously be manipulated in fundraising communication. Donors often prefer to concentrate on those categories of cause that they perceive either as most relevant to their segment of society, or more widely as supporting how they wish to see themselves, or have others see them.

The strength of the stimulus

A variety of authors have highlighted the importance of the strength of the stimulus generated by a particular charity. Tailoring the message to the target group can be particularly useful here, as can unique or original involvement devices that make an appeal stand out from the crowd and attract attention. The perceived urgency of the need can also make a difference. In general, high degrees of urgency would appear to engender high degrees of support. It would also appear that approaches which build up the degree of personal responsibility a donor might feel for a situation will be more effective at engendering a response. Other key variables warranting consideration under this general heading include the degree of personalisation attained in the communication and the clarity of the request. Clear and unambiguous requests for support are more likely to engender compliance than those that are vague or general in nature.

Why people do not support charities

Of course, no matter how good the communication, there will always be some individuals in society who will never respond to requests for cash donations, volunteering time, etc. Such individuals will simply ignore charity messages, because they have developed negative perceptions of the sector either *a priori* or as a result of some bad experience with an organisation they have supported in the past. Table 8.1 contains details of the primary reasons non-donors cite for not supporting the sector.

PROCESSING THE DEMAND FOR MONEY

Thus far into the model we have looked at the communications and messages that might be directed at prospective donors. We have also

Table 8.1 Common reasons for non-support

Reason given	%
I cannot afford to offer my support to charity.	23.3
Charities ask for inappropriate sums.	22.5
The government should fund the work undertaken by charities.	19.3
I find charity communications inappropriate.	12.0
The quality of service provided by charities to their donors is poor.	6.8
In the past charities have not acknowledged my support.	4.0
I feel that charities are not deserving.	2.8

(Reproduced by kind permission of the *International Journal of Nonprofit and Voluntary Sector Marketing*.)

looked at some of the mechanisms that might draw attention to these messages and bring these messages to the forefront of a prospective donor's mind, to the point where a decision must now be taken on whether to give or not.

Two key factors will influence the manner in which the giving decision is processed: the donor's past experience with a given charity (and with charitable giving in general), and the criteria that they might use to evaluate potential organisations for support.

Organisational performance

Considering, first, the issue of criteria used in decision making, chief among these is the question of organisational performance. This appears to act at two levels. First, we know that people who do not give to charities see them as being generally wasteful and inefficient. A typical non-donor believes that on average only around 45p in the £1 of a gift will actually be applied to the cause; the rest will be 'squandered' on fundraising and administration. For the donor, perceptions are somewhat more favourable, with a typical donor believing that around 65 per cent of any gift will be applied to the cause. When one considers that in reality it is well over 80 per cent (in most cases), a significant credibility gap appears to exist, even with supporters.

Performance may also act at the micro level. There is evidence that perceived efficiency can drive the choice of which specific organisation to support. It can also have a significant impact on the percentage of one's charitable 'pot' that might be allocated. There is therefore a link between perceived efficiency and the notion of 'donor lifetime value' – that is, the total amount that a particular supporter might donate over a number of years of regular gifts to the same charity. It is highly cost-effective to recruit a donor who will have a long-term relationship with a charity.

Impact on beneficiaries

In selecting an organisation to support, donors also care about the impact that their gift will have on beneficiaries. The extent to which an organisation is deemed effective is thus another important factor that may be reinforced through fundraising communications. So too are the benefits that might accrue from having made the gift. In general, research suggests that the stronger the desirability of any of these perceived benefits, the greater will be the likelihood of compliance and the total support engendered. The main types of benefit, or the 'utility' of gifts, are as follows:

- **Functional utility** – in the sense that an individual might support an organisation because they believe that the gift will have the desired impact on the beneficiary group.
- **Familial utility** – where giving is motivated by some personal link to the organisation or cause, perhaps through a friend or a loved one. The 'benefit' to the donor in the context is therefore emotional and grounded in personal relationships, be they past or present.
- **Demonstrable utility** – in the sense that the donor may derive some very tangible benefits from making a gift such as recognition, career enhancement, networking opportunities, or tax benefits.
- **Emotional utility** – where the utility derived is completely intangible and driven only by the donor's desire either to make a difference to a cause, or to alleviate what the psychologists would term a 'negative state' (ie to feel good about themselves).

Past experience of charity

A donor's past experience with a charity will also drive how they might behave in the future. There are primarily three factors that are at work here. The first concerns the quality of service provided by the fundraising department. Donors who describe themselves as 'very satisfied' with this service are twice as likely as those who describe themselves as merely 'satisfied' to make a second and subsequent gift. Donors expressing lower levels of satisfaction are significantly more likely to switch their giving to other organisations.

The second concerns the perceived responsiveness of the organisation. Those that listen carefully to the needs of their donors and make some attempt to match communications are likely to attract significantly higher levels of loyalty and/or gifts. At its simplest level this may involve ensuring that donors are not reciprocated with other charities against their wishes, that details are updated as requested, or that requests to avoid certain types of solicitation (such as telemarketing) are honoured. At a higher level of sophistication, this might involve tailoring communications to known donor interests and offering some flexibility in the type, nature and frequency of communications received. All such strategies have proven effects on loyalty.

The third concerns the perceived impact that past support has had on the cause. Pretty much any text on charity fundraising will stress the need to provide feedback to donors in respect of how their gift has been used, and yet comparatively few organisations actually make this happen in practice. We now understand from research that this factor does have an appreciable impact on donor behaviour, and charities neglect it at their peril.

CHARACTERISTICS THAT AFFECT INDIVIDUAL PERCEPTIONS OF CHARITIES AND THE VALUE OF GIVING

As the model in Figure 8.1 clearly illustrates, the manner in which charity appeals are perceived and the decision-making process conducted will both be influenced by a variety of demographic, cultural and personal characteristics. Each of these factors will now be considered in turn.

Demographic characteristics

The key category of external variables that determines donor behaviour is undoubtedly that of the demographic profile of the charity donor or prospective donor. The age of an individual would appear to be directly related to their propensity to both engage in charity giving and the level at which such behaviour will take place. It is estimated that some people aged 55–70 make 65 per cent of charitable gifts.

As noted in other chapters, younger generations appear in general to be less motivated to give to charity than would have previously been the case. Given this, it is no surprise that charities are experimenting with new media in an attempt to engage with a younger audience. Face-to-face solicitation has worked well for some, while others have looked to the new electronic media such as the internet or interactive television. At the time of writing, the jury is still out on whether such methods of recruitment will ultimately generate satisfactory lifetime values.

A variable related to the age of the prospective donor is that of 'life stage'. The motivation for giving to a number of charities, notably those connected in some way with medical research, may be related to a great extent to the level of involvement an individual might have with the problem addressed by a charity. Those individuals who either suffer from a particular complaint, or who are perhaps related to a sufferer, will be somewhat more disposed to giving than those that have no such association.

The variable 'gender' has also been shown to have a key impact on giving behaviour. There is evidence that women differ from men in their expectations of charity. Research in the discipline of psychology has shown us that women want precise explanations of how their money will be used and tend to prefer one-off donations to an on-going commitment. They also tend to give smaller amounts than men (although the gap is narrowing) and to support a wider range of organisations. In addition, women appear to give more 'from the heart than the head'. Some cancer charities, for example, have had success in developing gender-specific copy in their direct mail, directing facts, figures and research evidence towards their male audience, and human-interest case studies towards the female.

Not surprisingly, the variable 'social class/income' is also an important determinant of charitable behaviour. Lower socio-economic groups tend to see needy people as a group to be pitied because of their treatment at the hand of fate. Promotional messages stressing the ability of even a small gift to alleviate pain and suffering are therefore likely to be most effective. The higher socio-economic groups, by contrast, particularly those from the professions, give not only for the amelioration of suffering but also for the longer-term change in their situation. Support is thus prompted by a need to make a change in a social structure, and promotional messages could perhaps reflect this motivation.[1]

---

[1] For anyone specifically interested in the motives of higher-net-worth individuals, Paul Schervish working at Boston College in the USA has developed what he terms ten logics of philanthropy. For further information, visit his website on www.bc.edu.

Interestingly, we also know that poor and extremely wealthy people give a much higher proportion of their income than the middle class, and that those living in small town/rural settings are more willing to exhibit helping behaviours than city dwellers.

The personality of a given individual does not in general appear to be a good indicator of charity support. A number of studies have, however, highlighted that the self-confident are more likely to offer help than other categories of individual. There is also evidence that intrinsically motivated people do more for charity than self-centred, external-reward seekers.

A number of studies have in addition suggested that the existence of social norms may also be an issue. A significant percentage of philanthropic activity is motivated by normative concerns. People appear to pay considerable attention to what others contribute. Judgements in respect of giving are therefore made in terms of beliefs about what is normative for the group. The concept of group is of particular significance, since individuals perceive themselves as members of some groups, but not others. Since it was identified earlier that individuals would tend to support other individuals perceived as similar to themselves, the perception of group membership is key for fundraisers to understand and exploit in their solicitation activity. The self can be viewed as a series of abstract categories; thus, any attempt to understand the act of giving as an individual (behavioural) end point is likely to miss important features of what charity means in its fullest sense. Indeed, pressure to conform to the norms of behaviour expected by various societal groups has been explored in a number of studies, resulting in the derivation of group incentives where no individual incentive could previously be identified. Recent research suggests that the degree to which pressures of this type exist will affect compliance positively. People are significantly more likely to give if they feel pressure from reference groups such as friends and relatives. It is interesting to note, however, that this kind of pressure can negatively affect the longevity of the donor relationship, with this category of individual being substantially more likely to lapse when these pressures abate.

The topic of religion has also been widely explored in the literature and has been shown to be an important demographic factor in determining giving. It appears that those professing a religious faith are significantly more likely to support charity than those without such a belief. There is also a marked (albeit non-linear) relationship between the strength of that belief and the degree of support that will be proffered.

As a final note in this section, it is worth noting that what we have in effect been doing in the foregoing paragraphs is to delineate those characteristics that distinguish charity givers from non-givers. Research from NCVO and CAF confirms that those individuals who offer significant support to the sector comprise a very unique and distinguishable target group. The problem for many charities to address, however, is the extent to which their donor base might differ from that of another organisation. If this is the case, such knowledge can be used to inform the accurate targeting of prospective new donors and the content of any communications that might be used.

In deciding whether it is possible to 'segment' the donor market (ie to target an unique audience), it is necessary to distinguish demographic bases for segmentation from those based on lifestyle. Demographic criteria such as age, gender, socio-economic group generally are of very little use in distinguishing those donating to one organisation from those donating to another. Whether they are or are not of such use is a function of the breadth of programmes offered or the breadth of the recipient groups to whom benefit is offered. Those charities with a wide appeal are likely to appeal to an equally wide range of donors and will therefore find the demographic profile of their database to be very similar to other equally broad-based charities.

Even where this is the case, however, experience tells us that some organisations may still find it possible to segment the market on the basis of lifestyle. Lifestyle is simply an amalgam of someone's interests, opinions, hobbies/interests, media exposure, etc. These characteristics are often related to the nature of the cause (eg yachting, in the case of the RNLI), but not necessarily so. The RNID recently increased its response rate to cold mail by including the lifestyle characteristic 'enjoys gardening' in its criteria for the selection of 'cold' recruitment lists.

Personal characteristics

Intrinsic or personal determinants of charitable giving behaviour are those that address the underlying individual motives for electing to support a charity at a given level. They can assist donors in filtering out those charity appeals that are likely to be of most relevance and can help in structuring the evaluation process that they will subsequently conduct to define the pattern of support exhibited.

Key among these is the extent to which the donor feels empathy with the recipient. In general, it appears that the greater the degree of empathy that might be engendered, the stronger the likelihood that help will be offered. To be effective, however, creative treatments must be powerful enough to arouse empathy, but not so powerful that they become personally distressing to the donor.

The motive 'sympathy' has also received attention in the literature, largely being viewed as a means of expressing one's own values, aiding individuals to conform to personally held norms. Again, there would appear to be a relationship between the degree of sympathy engendered and both the propensity to donate and the chosen level of support. A variety of other potential motives for giving have been identified including fear, guilt and pity, which have been found to affect both compliance and the extent thereof.

Charity giving can of course be motivated by a giver's self-interest. Variables such as importance, self-esteem and recognition have often been identified as key motivations for charitable giving. There is also evidence that people will give if their belief in a just world is threatened. This is known as 'social justice theory' and generally suggests that helping behaviour would be increased when this is the case. We also know that this motive is particularly strong when the need is not widespread and the duration of the need (persistence) is short. It is interesting to note that most charity communications appear based on the exact opposite of this position. Appeals tend to stress the ongoing nature of the need for support and make much of the number of individuals currently being affected with the affliction/cause for concern.

A variety of different factors, therefore, have the capacity to affect charity giving behaviour. The factors are often complex and inter-related and suggest both altruistic and selfish motivations for giving.

RESULTS

The final dimension of the model concerns the result of the decision-making process. Charities tend in practice to be supported in a variety of different ways. Gifts may consist of monetary donations, gifts of time, or even gifts in kind. There are, however, two other key outputs from the model that must be considered. Donors can clearly elect to support their chosen charity at a variety of different levels. The share of a particular individual's expenditure will become an increasingly important variable for charities to consider, particularly in Britain where, as has been previously noted, the 'donor pool' has been shown to be contracting.

The concept of donor lifetime value has been shown to be affected by a variety of factors, many of which have been discussed previously in this chapter. The strongest predictors of overall value have been shown to be income, religion and variables within the charity's control, such as perceived efficiency, effectiveness, responsiveness, quality of communications and, in the case of some health charities, the degree of familial utility that might be derived from a gift.

It is interesting to consider these factors alongside the reasons donors actually give for attrition. These are presented in Table 8.2. Particularly noteworthy here is the fact that a high proportion of donors simply elect to switch their support to other organisations. It is also interesting to note the percentage of lapsed supporters who cannot remember having supported the organisation in the first place. Both reasons for lapse suggest that relationship failures are common within the sector, and attendance to many of the issues highlighted above would therefore seem likely to enhance levels of loyalty.

Uncommitted givers (individuals giving a series of single donations) tend at present to remain loyal to an organisation for a period of no more than five years, with a 50 per cent attrition rate normally being experienced between the first and second donation. Committed givers tend to remain loyal for somewhat longer, but even here the duration of the relationship tends to extend no further than six to seven years. There are thus significant opportunities to develop extant levels of loyalty. Indeed, as charities gain a more detailed understanding of the lifetime value of their donors, it seems likely that the success of

Table 8.2 Reasons given by donors for no longer supporting organisations (%)

Reason	%
I feel that other causes are more deserving.	26.5
I can no longer afford to offer my support to this organisation.	22.3
No memory of ever supporting.	11.4
Still supporting by other means.	6.8
Moved home.	6.7
I found the organisation's communications inappropriate.	3.6
Not reminded to give again.	3.3
The organisation asked for inappropriate sums.	3.1
The organisation did not inform me how my money had been used.	1.7
The organisation no longer needs my support.	1.2
The organisation did not acknowledge my support.	0.9
The quality of service provided by the organisation was poor.	0.9
The organisation did not take account of my wishes.	0.7
Staff at the organisation were unhelpful.	0.5

fundraising activity may in the future be measured, not only by the immediate returns that it generates, but also by changes in the length of donor relationships over time.

FINAL THOUGHTS

In this chapter, many potential influences on donor behaviour have been explored, drawn largely from the academic literature. This list is not exhaustive and is intended only as an overview of a very complex subject. Nevertheless, a greater understanding of the variables in the model postulated in this chapter would undoubtedly help charities focus their efforts on those individuals most likely to offer some form of support. Enhanced opportunities for donor targeting, based perhaps on the extrinsic determinants of giving behaviour highlighted in this paper, should serve to greatly reduce the costs of a given donor recruitment programme. Moreover, as organisations begin to understand how information is processed by donors and the intrinsic determinants of behaviour, charities can more effectively tailor the messages contained in their promotional appeals to add relevance for their potential new donors and those who have given previously to the organisation.

More generally, in other forms of both personal and non-personal communications, charities would be advised to consider the processing determinants that will be used in reaching an ultimate decision in respect of whether or not a particular donation will be made. A donor's past experience with a charity and their satisfaction with the standard of service received will clearly have a relevance here, as will the judgmental criteria that will be employed to select between the charitable options available to them. Charity branding, annual reports, media coverage and the overall profile of an organisation all have the capacity to enhance or detract from the evaluations that donors make against these criteria.

In assessing what drives prospective donors and donors to behave in a particular way, our model of giving behaviour can be used as a framework to develop as comprehensive a list of factors as possible. Many of these will be organisation-specific, and the significance of their impact will clearly vary. The model can, however, be used as a framework to ensure that all relevant factors are considered, and understanding can be deepened through research before a fundraising campaign is developed. Otherwise, we as fundraisers run the risk of alienating our audience or, perhaps even worse, failing to engage with the boundless enthusiasm that many still feel for our sector.

Select bibliography

For further reading on the effects of fundraising techniques on donors' behaviour, and contributions from social psychology, see also:

Benson P L and Catt V L (1978) 'Soliciting Charity Contributions: the parlance of asking for money', *Journal Of Applied Social Psychology*, **8:** 84–95.

Burnett J J and Wood V R (1988) 'A Proposed Model of the Donation Process', *Research in Consumer Behaviour*, **3:**1–47.

Cann A, Sherman S J, and Elkes R (1975) 'Effects Of Initial Request Size and Timing of a Second Request On Compliance: the foot in the door and the door in the face', *Journal of Personality and Social Psychology*, **32**: 774–782.

Cialdini R B and Schroeder D A (1976) 'Increasing Compliance By Legitimising Paltry Contributions: when even a penny helps', *Journal Of Personality and Social Psychology*, **34**: 599–604.

Dixon M (1997) 'Small and Medium Sized charities Need A Strong Brand Too: crisis experience', *Journal Of Nonprofit and Voluntary Sector Marketing*, **2**(1): 52–57.

Greenlee J S and Gordon T P (1997) 'The Impact of Professional Solicitors on Fund Raising in Charitable Organisations', paper presented to *ARNOVA conference*, Indianapolis, December.

Haggberg M (1992) 'Why Donors Give', *Fund Raising Management*, **23** (2): 39–40.

Hibbert S A and Horne S (1996) 'Giving To Charity: questioning the donor process', *The Journal Of Consumer Marketing*, **13**(2): 4–13.

Lovelock C H and Weinberg C B (1984) *Marketing For Public and Nonprofit Managers*. New York: John Wiley and Sons.

Piliavin J A and Charng H W (1990) 'Altruism: a review of recent theory and research', *Annual Review Of Sociology*, **16**: 27–65.

Radley A and Kennedy M (1995) 'Charitable Giving By Individuals: a study of attitudes and practice', *Human Relations*, **48**(6): 685–709.

Sargeant A and McKenzie J (1998*) A Lifetime Of Giving: an analysis of donor lifetime value*. West Malling: CAF.

Weyant J M (1984) 'Applying Social Psychology To Induce Charitable Donations', *Journal Of Applied Social Psychology*, **14**: 441–447.

For complete references to the research mentioned in this chapter, see Sargeant A (1999) 'Charity Giving: towards a model of donor behaviour', *Journal of Marketing Management*, **15**: 215–238. See also Sargeant A, West D C and Ford J B (2001) 'The Role of Perceptions in Predicting Donor Value', *Journal of Marketing Management* **17**: 407–428.

In this chapter, some aspects of the future for giving are mapped out, including the legal framework, globalisation, the role of new media and a new contract for the relationship between charities and donors that reflects significant social change as we go into the twenty-first century. In the following (and final) chapter of the book, the main messages emerging from the body of material in this book are pulled together by the editors, who present their own vision of the main challenges facing all those involved in sustaining individual giving and the unique role of charities in meeting society's needs.

THE CREDIBILITY OF CHARITY   Richard Fries

For charity to attract giving it has to be credible – and credible not just to those involved day to day with charity but to the ordinary member of the public who gives in response to appeals, or who would give if convinced of its value. One of the factors necessary for charities to be credible is that people have to believe that what they give is properly used, and this requires the right sort of accountability and supervision. These are issues that go beyond the scope of this contribution, which is concerned with the even more fundamental issue of whether the idea of charity as such continues to have the right sort of resonance with ordinary people; whether, that is, the ethos of charity as now practised reflects people's idea of what charity should be.

It is notorious, at least to those who know something of charity law, that there is a large gulf between the public's notion of charity and the legal definition and the legal technicalities of charity. This matters because the goodwill and confidence that attach to charity play a crucial role in promoting giving. The giving public does not need to know, or even to be able to understand, the detailed technicalities of charity law; but it does have to have confidence that the law reflects a philanthropic vision which it shares. In the last century charity came, in certain circles at least, to have a bad name, a reputation for condescension, even for heartlessness ('cold charity'). It is the claim of our common-law tradition that charity does match the public vision, and does move with the changing times, needs and attitudes. How does the reality measure up to the claim?

That public confidence cannot be taken for granted is manifest in the findings of surveys and other evidence of public opinion. People continue to give to charity, but not all are convinced that the money goes to the stated purpose, or at any rate a sufficient proportion – with only the bare minimum diverted to administration and other 'unproductive' purposes. Behind this scepticism lies the ambiguous jibe that 'charities are no better than businesses' – begging the question of the extent to which business values, and efficiency in particular, are or are not appropriate for charity.

Since charity ranges from the National Trust to your local parent teacher association, from ancient almshouses to new community groups, public confusion is understandable. To talk of charity, or the charitable sector, in the singular is misleading, creates false expectations of a detailed common nature and ethos which is illusory. It would actually be damaging if all charities had to submit to a single detailed template. A common mistake is to judge one part of the charitable sector by the standards proper to another. A multimillion-pound 'business' cannot be run like a community organisation.

Yet there is an abiding identity in charity, renewed and developed in the light of changing circumstances, but resting on basic principles of continuing validity. These have recently been reaffirmed by the McFadden Commission, set up by the Scottish Executive to reform charity law and regulation in Scotland. The McFadden report defines charity as that which is in the public interest, independent, non-profit distributing and non-political. These four principles underlie charity. That the arrangements for determining what constitutes charity, and for holding charities to these principles, should be credible to the public is what is necessary for public confidence, and therefore for public giving. This is what underlies the recommendations in the McFadden report.

The notion of public benefit lies at the heart of charity. Indeed, recent reports, from the Deakin Commission (NCVO, 1996) to NCVO's Working Group (2001), have focused reform on making public benefit the essential test, stripping away the qualifications and presumptions of centuries of court judgements. In the diverse modern world, agreement on what constitutes the public benefit is hardly to be had – there is bound to be disagreement, for example about what forms of health care, of education, of religion are in the public interest, and therefore ought to qualify automatically for the tax privileges and public reputation that charitable status brings.

So the mechanism and authority for determining charitable status is important. On the face of it a new framework, designed for the twenty-first century, must be preferable to a 400-year-old text – the preamble to the long-repealed Charitable Uses Act of 1601, as modified and interpreted by the courts, and latterly by the Charity Commission, over the years. A review of how that framework should be constituted is long overdue and has at last been instigated by the government's Performance and Innovation Unit (PIU), which aims to enable the development of new types of organisation and ensure public confidence in the sector. Meanwhile we depend on the Charity Commission to use the authority the courts have given to develop the scope of charity responsibly but progressively. The Commission has a long tradition of approaching new issues flexibly and positively, from the adoption of race relations as a charitable purpose in the 1980s to the systematic review that it is undertaking now. The Commission Review of the Register has already shown the capacity of the existing arrangements to respond to such modern needs and practices as urban and rural regeneration and community development.

These issues highlight the changing approach to the ethos of charity. The old conception of charity as the fortunate helping the needy has long since become anachronistic. Self-help, which used to be the preserve of the parallel tradition of mutualism, now informs the charitable ethos. That beneficiaries should be involved in the running of charities is well accepted, and reflected in the interpretation the Charity Commission gives of charity law. Similarly, the notion that charities may engage in enterprise, exploiting opportunities for commercial activity in pursuit of their charitable purpose, is accepted, even where there is an element of private gain provided that is subsidiary. And that charities have a right, even a duty, to campaign in support of their charitable purpose is well established.

The combination of change and the pressures that partnership with government and obtaining funding have put on voluntary action have pushed many bodies that are arguably beyond the boundaries of what charity should embrace to seek charitable status. Alongside groups with a general public purpose, society also benefits from community groups devoted primarily to the interests of its members, and from enterprises seeking to make a profit and thereby enrich deprived areas. In addition to the development of our concepts of what deserves charitable status and constitutes charity, we need to modernise co-operatives and mutuals.

That a review of the legal and regulatory framework for charities and the voluntary sector is being carried out by the PIU shows that the government takes these issues seriously. At the time of writing we await with interest how this initiative will develop.

A MEMORANDUM ON THE GLOBALISATION OF FUTURE PHILANTHROPY   David Wickert

One word should be added to every prediction you hear about the future of charity. The word is *international*.

Philanthropy in the twentieth century started with the wealthy few (Cadbury, Carnegie, Ford, Rockefeller). In the twenty-first century, it will continue what has already started and become both increasingly egalitarian and international thanks to the internet, and to whatever may eventually succeed the internet. The global activities of the media and financial institutions, companies and governments and, most importantly of all, the increasingly diverse character of populations, the experiences of ordinary people as they travel to different parts of the world are significant for the future shape of philanthropy: the donor base will be increasingly global. This should lead to an increase in cross-border fundraising and cross-border funding. The choice that donors want most is the choice of the project or programme that their donation is going to support; it will matter less and less where the charity is based. The important thing will be whether their donations will make an impact wherever intervention is needed. Donors will not only depend on the well-known international agencies or charities to channel support and programmes to developing countries or areas where disaster relief is needed. They will be able, through the internet, to access information, interaction and online donation facilities with charities directly, wherever they are.

Electronic communications are opening global philanthropic markets. One implication of the increased transparency and choice that this entails is that charities will have to work together to eliminate unacceptable overlap and duplication in their missions, client groups and areas of operation. And, as the relationship between the charity and the donor evolves and develops, so will the need for the charity manager to think internationally. Executives will be expected to have management expertise, technological experience and a global view of change.

'We are going to see more philanthropic activity and advocacy work, all the things we mean by civil society, happening globally,' says Professor Dennis Young, President of the Association for Research on Non-Profit Organisations. Internet globalisation will make donors and trustees of charities and non-profit organisations increasingly aware of where the needs are. Their judgements will be directly informed by individuals in need.

This will end philanthropic isolationism. Non-profit resources will be focused on where they are needed most, not be 'restricted' to the country where the funds are raised. Of course, in many instances there is no actual 'restriction' on where funds are used. But there is, for example in the USA, a natural conservatism among trustees and donors that is neatly summed up in the words: Charity begins at home. And in other countries (eg in South Africa) there are actual restrictions.

A result of this is a demand for a change in the rules about tax advantages for donations. Currently, where tax advantages are available, they are designed to benefit domestic charities. In some countries, for example in the USA, it is legally possible, under the rules, for domestic benefits to be extended to charities in other countries, but the process is often complicated and adds to costs.

Because charitable and non-profit activity is so significant across the world, there is increasing pressure for it to have some real international recognition. Governments' and other international bodies' praise of charities' efforts is mere froth if they do not encourage their citizens to support them. An international agreement framed in a way acceptable to a majority of governments may not be far off. The agreement might, for example, mean that every country sets a certain minimum sum (say up to the local equivalent of US$250) that can be given away by each taxpayer tax-free, and *to any eligible non-profit organisation anywhere in the world*. The minimum could be higher at the discretion of the national government concerned. The definition of 'any non-profit organisation' could be decided country by country by each national government, and each non-profit that qualified would be given a straightforward way of demonstrating its status that would be internationally recognised. The minimum would be set low so that the loss of tax would not cripple national economies. The effect of this would be that taxpayers across the world would have a small incentive to support charities nationally and internationally.

Global donor populations open up immense opportunities for charities. They need to be ready to do global business!

THE DONOR–CHARITY DEAL John Kingston

Charities are in the business of changing the world. Increasingly, this will not be through the supply of elastoplast, but the prevention of the injury, the banning of the weapon. The challenge will not be the communication of a winning brand, product or service to donors and supporters – it will be the successful selling of a vision, the charity's own vision of change. It will be the building of a constituency, even a movement, which will promote a change that will better our society.

While charities will want donors to buy into this long-term commitment to sustainable change, donors with unlimited access to new media and daily evidence of global challenges will also become increasingly aware that there are no 'magic bullets' for deep-rooted, complex social problems. They will be looking for ideas, vision and strategic thinking about those problems. The future generation of donors will be less persuaded by fundraising that promises instant solutions, and less content with action directed only at palliative relief of the casualties of failing social policy, whether local, national or global.

Charities must respect that donors may be sophisticated or emotional, or indeed both – passion and professionalism are not mutually exclusive! Whatever the donors' starting point, the role of a charity will be to educate and engage them in what the charity is trying to achieve, to invite partnership in those ambitions and to work together with those donors – and their gifts of time, commitment and money – to change the world.

There are three strands to this evolutionary process: for donors, a commitment to invest in sustainable change; for charities, more movement to advocacy alongside action; and for both, new mechanisms to resource programmes of work.

Donors as investors in sustainable change

Charities will want to recruit donors to become partners who wish to invest in sustainable change, rather than to contribute to one-off projects, short-term fire fighting or crisis relief – although this latter support, of course, will still have a role to play in emergency situations.

For example, Save the Children is investing in recruiting supporters who share their vision for children – a world that takes children seriously. Save the Children is calling for a similar shift in our approach and attitude to children as that which has dramatically occurred in Britain in our attitude to the environment and the role of women.

It is naïve to think that such fundamental change is easy, or speedy. Charities will need to explain to existing supporters the length of the journey ahead, and to recruit new donors who also appreciate the timescales involved.

The growing interest in venture philanthropy is encouraging. We should welcome donors who want to see strategic plans, who will invest in core costs, who want to measure progress against targets – donors who want to build sustainable voluntary enterprise.

More advocacy and campaigning

There is an old story … A man was standing by a river. A baby came floating down in the water. He jumped in and saved it. And another. And another. He then walked up the river, to stop the person who was throwing the children into the water. Palliative service delivery – action to tackle root causes. A further twist to the story could be the launching of a campaign or a movement that aimed to make the act of throwing children into the water totally unacceptable, a behaviour that became entirely unnatural to all in society. Advocacy and campaigning – changing the world …

As more charities develop beyond service delivery to advocacy and campaigning, the fundraisers face new challenges. How to recruit and develop support for the vision, when the 'need–action–benefit' fundraising methodology is so deeply rooted in the minds and behaviour of trustees, fundraising directors and supporters? How to aim to find recruits to the movement, without undermining the tried and tested fundraising mechanisms that bring in the money to pay for infrastructure and core costs?

The fundraising message must be totally on mission, and the mission explainable in succinct, clear terms to a variety of audiences. A three-page mission statement will reflect a lack of clear thinking! And charities will have to continue to grapple with measuring impact, targets and milestones, rather than relying on measures of input, such as voluntary income, to demonstrate effective performance.

New mechanisms, new wealth, new donors

Tomorrow's potential donors live in a society of investors, whether these be pensions, equities, insurance policies, ISAs or cash deposits. The invitation to invest in social capital, that is programmes or projects with a social return, should provide the opportunity to attract a group of people already used to calculating the difference between short- and long-term returns, unlikely to place their resources anywhere unless the rewards are clear.

There is a pool of very wealthy and relatively 'mass affluent' individuals in Britain and globally, with the capacity to make serious contributions to philanthropy. Committed givers have always been important to charities, and they will become more so as charities' programmes become more visionary. Charities must not miss the chance to capitalise on these resources by ensuring that what they have on offer is presented in a way that appeals to this growing market. Society's winners will want the charities they support to win. Charities will need to get smart in their marketing to these people.

Additionally, the polar divide between 'philanthropy' and 'profit' will begin to disappear. This divide is perhaps illustrated by the current orthodoxy practised by many charitable foundations, which invest their endowment in the stock market (profit) and give the annual yield to charities (philanthropy), but find it difficult to consider investing income or capital in opportunities in the range between the two extremes (ie where a lower commercial return is complemented by a social return, or where a voluntary project benefits from the use of financial instruments, such as long-term debt). As David Carrington (of the UK Social Investment Taskforce) has put it, 'Stop investing in Mayfair, and giving the rent to the poor of Hackney. Start investing in Hackney!'

A number of initiatives are under way to break down the polarisation, including:

* Charity Commission guidelines (May 2001) on the use of debt and other financial instruments to support voluntary enterprise;
* the drive for Social Responsible Investment by mainstream investors (including charities);
* the possible launch of Charity Bank in Spring 2002;
* work to develop social venture capital (for example, the Beacon Fund, CAF's Risk Investment Fund).

What does it all mean?

No one is saying that achieving social change is an easy business. That does not mean that charities will not attract support for a visionary proposition. New donor-investors will want to invest in a different kind of future for society, and not just provide a penny in the bucket for the vulnerable. They will look to invest in people and organisations explicitly addressing new agendas for change. Charities will need to show how gifts can leverage resources, outlining to donors, for example, a three-year programme and indicating how they can help at the different milestones along the way.

Higher investment from these donors is not likely to be achieved without the dedication of higher resources from charities and others. The donors of the future will need access to good information, advice and data. A tiny but burgeoning donor advice profession in Britain reflecting this need is growing, including initiatives such as Project Connect. 'Donor advisers' are likely to represent a powerful strand in the changing fundraising market, and charities will need to be ready to engage.

The future is uncertain, full of risk and opportunity. Those engaged in promoting these changes in the resourcing of the voluntary sector are in for a bumpy ride. But it will be exciting, and it will undoubtedly lead to substantial and positive change over the next ten years.

THE ELECTRONIC FUTURE   Sarah Hughes

Technology provides us with a glimpse of what the future might hold. It is possible to imagine, for example, a world of interactive TV, where we could click in and out of programmes, e-mails and websites; in fact much of this is already becoming a reality. But what of a world in which the latest news could be received via any screen, in any room of our homes? What if that news could automatically be supported by a live programme from a charity working in the field? As events unfold, how easy would it be for households to come together in making a donation to that charity through their TV set?

The future of technology lies in its ubiquity: information will be everywhere, on screens, on billboards and neon signs, on hand-held gadgets, and on home appliances: wherever we want it to be. Charities will need to become as ubiquitous as the technology that serves them. They will need to revolutionise both their branding and their online activities if they are to succeed in the dynamic world of the 'virtual' charity.

They will have to become proficient in disseminating vast amounts of knowledge in manageable, tailored chunks. And, as donors glide between different sources of information, they will be making considered decisions about which charity to support, and balancing subjectivity with objectivity. In fact, these patterns of behaviour are already emerging, guided by the accessibility of information through the internet.

Once donors act, however, they will expect not only a rapid response but also an account of how their money has been used, and a measure of the impact of their donation. They will expect their own actions to result in change, and they will ask the charities they support to set realistic, attainable targets.

Donors themselves will change. Already, young donors are bucking the long-term decline in their numbers, and showing a great willingness to donate online. Increasingly, they will come to represent the spectrum of society, with each expecting charities to deliver a personal, tailored service, cost-effectively. Some will donate; some will invest first and donate later; others will seek to buy a stake in the charity itself; and micro-money will become as important as major gifts.

In turn, charities will have to become proficient in their e-business. By linking together their people, systems and processes, they will be able to present a seamless set of choices to the donor, choices based around busy lifestyles and an insistence on convenience.

Above all, giving will be interactive. Donors will want to be empowered by the process, from whatever moved them to give in the first place to the impact and consequences of their support. Meanwhile, charities will be forced to bring donors into closer contact with the causes, issues and projects they have chosen to support. Ultimately, charities will become society's great educators and a leading influence on human behaviour.

They also have a key role to play in the global community. As the sense of social responsibility is heightened, so too is the desire for knowledge, and an understanding of issues that were previously beyond the area of interest for most people. With teams living and working in some of the worst-affected regions, charities will be uniquely placed to provide this information – as long as they have the right technology.

Already, fieldworkers are able to send digital images or live webcasts back to their offices, so is it such a great leap to send these images direct to a self-selected group of donors? Or, for that matter, for the donors themselves to be able to direct a camera in the field to achieve their own view of activities?

So, far from creating a culture of 'couch potato' giving, technology will engage, stimulate and involve donors in the whole charitable process. And, as paper gives way to sound and images, so charities will empower their donors to see, to experience and, above all, to act for themselves.

THE FUTURE OF CIVIL SOCIETY   Barry Knight

If you have come here to help me, you are wasting your time.
But if you have come because your liberation is bound up with mine, then let us work together.
(Lilla Watson, Brisbane-based Aboriginal educator and activist)

The changing face of giving

Patterns of giving are changing. They have changed before, and they will change again. In the ancient Mediterranean world, private wealth brought with it a host of civic duties, and generosity was a political necessity rather than an inner moral virtue (Smith and Borgmann, 2001). Later, the religious impulse became more important, and was the driving force behind nineteenth-century philanthropy (Beveridge, 1948). In the twentieth century with the rise of secular social action, public altruism took over, reaching its apotheosis in the mid-1980s with Band Aid, telethons, and fun events (Knight, 1993).

The change that is taking place now is towards a strategic investment model of giving. The leitmotif of this is venture-based philanthropy producing public benefit through social entrepreneurship (Reiss and Clohesy, 2001). Such a development is likely to transform the philanthropic and non-profit sector very rapidly. Already in the United Kingdom, the old notion of charity, with its separation of benefactor and beneficiary, may be on the way out. Self-help groups may be included in a new definition of charity if proposals by the Commission on Scottish Charity Law Reform are accepted. Similar reviews of charity law are underway in England and Wales, and may shortly be announced in Northern Ireland.

Why is this taking place?

Changes are occurring at three levels. First, at the macro level, there is a huge change in 'global' patterns of wealth creation, demographics, technology, and patterns of social interaction. Second, at the micro level, there are 'local' changes in consciousness of individuals and how people make up their worldviews. Third, at the meso level (that is, the intermediary level where these trends converge), institutions in the public, private, and voluntary sectors are being buffeted by forces that they barely understand and to which they are doing their best to respond, without being sure how to.

Macro changes

The great drivers of change are burgeoning wealth among the expanding middle classes and the polarisation of society into 'haves' and 'have-nots'. There is the famous inter-generational transfer of wealth shortly to take place as the baby boomers inherit their parents' estates. Down the track, the echo-baby boomers will inherit the baby boomers' wealth. This means that excess wealth will be concentrated in the hands of the middle classes, while the needs of those who are currently poor are likely to get even greater (Institute of Fiscal Studies, 2001).

These trends mean that the amount of resources available to give away will be much larger, but that the needs are likely to be much larger too. It is becoming increasingly clear, and will become much more so in the next two or three years, that traditional charity is not enough. A new generation of entrepreneurs who are responsible for the creation of this new wealth is beginning to talk a new language of social enterprise (Reiss and Clohesy, 2001), while some experienced philanthropists are beginning to talk about a 'new civic gospel' (Adams, 2001).

Micro changes

Turning from the global to the local, the views of ordinary individuals are vital to the future of giving. Research conducted on individual donors shows that there are major psychological complexities involved in giving (Morrison, 1999), but that it is possible to construct types of donor. In the study, based on 2,000 questionnaires, motivations for giving were investigated and detailed maps drawn of how a sub-sample of 41 people saw giving.

The study concluded that individual giving had little to do with age, gender, class or other demographic characteristics. What was most significant was the belief system of the individual. What tended to unite individuals was their perception of themselves as investors.

Meso changes

Macro trends and micro trends appear to be converging. Between the global and the local, it is in the middle that all of the stress between the macro and the micro changes are likely to get played out. Here the definition of 'meso' (or 'middle') is the institutions that have to deal with problems on a day-to-day basis: governments, companies, and the charities and voluntary bodies that form civil society.

At both the macro and the micro level, trends are pushing giving towards investment. Essentially, this means that donors want to see a return on their money. This has enormous implications for the charities that are charged with the responsibility of enacting the wishes of their donors.

If they are to keep their donors, charities are going to have to become more efficient and effective and also be able to demonstrate gains in these respects. The charitable sector has been somewhat insulated from criticism in the past. Critics have been few – the occasional cool look at the sector by *The Economist* and the biting criticisms from Polly Toynbee in her *Guardian* columns have for the most part been ignored by the sector. But this is all set to change as the charitable sector comes under increasing scrutiny.

Why is this so? The answer goes back 20 years, to a time when serious concerns about the condition of public services began to be voiced (Hadley and Hatch, 1981). Reform of the public services began in earnest with the Financial Management Initiative of 1982, which used the term 'Value for Money' to assess public expenditure. The term 'Best Value' replaced this in 1997 when the Labour government came to power, but the ideas were essentially similar. In the past three or four years – beginning with a Social Exclusion Unit Report (1998) – criticism of the public services has mounted, and the issue dominated the 2001 general election.

While these trends have occurred in the public services, the voluntary sector has gained in status. The highly influential Deakin Report (1996) has led to a 'compact' between the government and the voluntary sector, with rights and responsibilities on both sides. It follows from these arrangements that not only does the government have to deliver for the voluntary sector, but also the voluntary sector has to deliver for the government. As a corollary, for a seat at the top table, the voluntary sector has to demonstrate its 'value added' for society. This is a new and important challenge for the voluntary sector. Along with this new status will come more sophisticated criticisms about performance. Some recent critics have suggested that voluntary organisations have much to do to make the grade (Edwards, 2000).

Harnessing the power of giving

Charities need to get closer to, and work on the desires of, their donors. From evidence given here, it is clear that there is a rich stream of philanthropy that sees investment in the future as the keynote. To respond to this, charities need to work more on the society that donors want. This involves a complete change from the traditional role of charity, which performs a 'defensive' function in enabling people in need to contend with the situation that they found themselves in (Narayan, 2000), towards a 'transformative' function, which is necessary if the conditions that create the need are to be removed. Taking this theme further, Knight et al (2002) interviewed 10,000 citizens in 47 countries and developed a model of 'a good society' based on three interlocking forces. A good society occurs when people are able to fulfil their requirements for basic needs, association, and participation.

This three-fold ambition would be an appropriate vision for the charitable sector. It should do its best to ensure that: people's basic needs are met; people have appropriate means of meeting together to develop social bonds; and they have adequate say in the political issues in their lives. This vision, though simple, is what citizens say that they want, and it is what donors are likely to respond to. The charitable sector does not have to do all this itself; rather, it should ensure that the jobs are done by the most appropriate agency.

Such a vision involves putting a positive image of society forward, rather than working on the traditional deficit models that the charitable sector is predicated upon. This is a radical change of mind-set, and would involve organisations re-thinking the ways that they operate in the public domain. At present, different interests in the charitable sector compete with other interests for funds, and the outcome is division between different organisations and a weakened sector and society.

Organised giving has an important role to play here. Charitable foundations are one of the few sources of free money: so long as they abide by the law, they can fund whatever they like. Instead of following their current practice – funding umpteen projects in each of several categories – they should take a more strategic view of the society that we want, and fund it. Instead of funding 'projects', which are essentially inputs, they should decide what outcomes they want, and decide how to get them.

Good funders are therefore strategic. They decide the impact that they want to have and tailor all grant making to outcomes that support the impact. It follows that they will fund long-term. They stick with an organisation for 20 to 30 years, keeping faith with those that deliver on the desired outcomes. They will fund, without any questions, activities such as organising, public policy advocacy, and coalition building, as long as they make a real difference. They fund core-operating costs. They put money into an organisation for capacity building without specifying how it is to be spent, but concentrating their assessments on whether the organisation delivers on the desired outcomes. They put money into evaluation, so that people know where we are on the social progress that we want.

This will put an end to the present sense of muddling along and vaguely doing good. What was good enough for the charitable sector in the twentieth century will not meet the demands of the twenty-first.

References

Adams E (2001) 'Enlargement, commitment, and a civil gospel: is there a future for philanthropy?' CENTRIS working paper. Newcastle upon Tyne: CENTRIS.

Beveridge W (1948) *Voluntary Action: a report on a means of social advance*. London: George Allen and Unwin.

Commission for the Future of the Voluntary Sector (1996) *Meeting the Challenge of Change: voluntary action into the 21st century (the Deakin Report)*. London: NCVO.

Edwards M (2000) *NGO Rights and Responsibilities: a new deal for global governance*. London: The Foreign Policy Studies Centre and NCVO.

Hadley R and Hatch S (1981) *Social Welfare and the Failure of the State*. London: George Allen and Unwin.

Institute of Fiscal Studies (2001) 'Inequality and living standards in Great Britain: some facts', *Institute of Fiscal Studies Briefing Note 19*. London: IFS.

Knight B (1993) *Voluntary Action*. London: Home Office.

Knight B, Chigudu H and Tandon R (2002 at press) *Reviving Democracy: citizens at the heart of governance*. London: Earthscan.

Morrison C (1999) *Donor Motivation*. Newcastle upon Tyne: Profunding.

Narayan D (2000) *Voices of the Poor: can anyone hear us?* New York: Oxford University Press for the World Bank.

NCVO (2001) *For the Public Benefit? A consultation document on charity law reform*. London: NCVO.

Reiss T and Clohesy S (2001) 'Unleashing New Resources and Entrepreneurship for the Common Good: a philanthropic renaissance' in Schluter A, Then V and Walkenhorst P (eds) *The Foundation Sector in Europe*. London: Directory of Social Change and CAF.

Smith J and Borgmann K (2001) 'Foundations in Europe: the historical context' in Schluter A, Then V and Walkenhorst P (eds) *The Foundation Sector in Europe*. London: Directory of Social Change and CAF.

Social Exclusion Unit (1998) *Bringing Britain Together*. London: Cabinet Office.

END-NOTE: RE-DEFINING CHARITY
Cathy Pharoah, Catherine Walker,
Pauline Jas and Andrew Passey

This book did not set out to explore or create any grand theory of giving but simply to map the state of individual giving and its relationship to charities today. Nonetheless the body of material that has been compiled, whether based on systematic research or the 'everyday' experience of those working in the field, presents a collective sense of the need for some radical changes in the context of charitable giving, the role of charity, and in the methods of fundraising. While the general concept of charity itself appears to have remained a relatively stable notion in spite of many significant social changes, such as declining patterns of church attendance, it has certainly not attracted the post-modern 'redefining' that has taken place in, for example, our thinking about urban regeneration, or joined-up government. With the government's Performance and Innovation Unit currently carrying out a review of voluntary sector law and regulation, this seems to be good time to ask 'What is modern charity? Is it cool to give?'

As Cathy Pharoah has set out in Chapter 3, the main data sources on giving reveal that the proportion of the population giving to charity has been falling since the mid-1990s, and levels of giving have only been maintained because existing donors are making larger average donations. The last decade of the twentieth century saw little significant growth in the overall level of giving to charity by the general population, although it was a decade in which many saw a considerable rise in their personal disposable income. It has been suggested by different authors throughout this book that the decline of participation in giving is in some way related to the lack of new thinking about the role of individual giving. The emergence of interest in venture philanthropy could be seen as one response to this crisis.

A parallel growth in wealth in the USA has led to very large increases in giving. The two most important explanations for these national differences are the differences in the tax reliefs available for individual donations in the two countries, and the contrasting cultures surrounding giving. In the USA, major gifts and endowments are publicly acknowledged and rewarded as important acts of citizenship. Against a background of faith in individual effort and a dislike of taxation and government intervention, private philanthropy has flourished. This culture is promoted by a tax system that rewards donations through major income tax reliefs.

In Britain, attitudes surrounding charitable giving are less clear-cut. Recent governments have shown a great willingness to promote individual giving through tax reliefs, with a growing emphasis on the return of tax directly to donors, but the climate for giving is problematic. Charities have been able to draw on a traditional fund of goodwill and general faith in the value of giving, but the foundations of the notion of charity itself have begun to require some underpinning. Generations brought up in a welfare democracy do not regard access to basic welfare provision as a matter of charity, but as one of rights. There have been other negative feelings about dependence on charity – that philanthropic funding comes with strings attached, or indicates a failure to do business profitably or to attract funding from more prestigious sources. Although this climate has not dried up the sources of philanthropy, it has certainly not encouraged it to thrive and grow out of ethical or ideological commitment.

To maintain and expand charity incomes, charity fundraisers have turned to the use of increasingly sophisticated marketing techniques modelled on the commercial sector, and many fear that such tactics are now beginning to backfire. Many of the commentators in this book have expressed anxiety about the medium- to long-term impact on donors of these approaches. Moreover, as John Kingston and others have pointed out, donors are increasingly discriminating about what charities can achieve. It has become critical to attend to the meaning that people attach to their charitable giving, to understand their expectations. This is no easy challenge. Supporting homeless people provides a rich territory of meanings. Does the public see homeless people as a group who have refused the appropriate help and services available, or as a community of those whose needs have been ignored? Can they best be helped through a gift of fifty pence, fifty pounds, by purchasing the *Big Issue*, providing an information leaflet about the nearest shelter, or making a phone-call to the local social work department? Does carrying puppies or children make homeless people a more appealing or appropriate cause for help? What significance does a ragged or neat appearance have? Are people embarrassed into making a gift, or happy to help a fellow citizen in need? Is it the role of charities to provide temporary relief for homeless people or to make inroads into the problem of homelessness?

There is no single answer to any of this. What has become clear from this volume is that charitable giving is not one single act or 'behaviour' but, instead, covers a range of different activities from spontaneous donations of a few pence in a pub collection, major donations of thousands of pounds, regular giving to favourite causes through direct debits or covenants, and 'events fundraising' such as schemes whereby individuals raise their own sponsorship to take part in, for example, international cycle trips to developing countries. The evidence pulled together by Pauline Jas and by Les Hems in their contributions show how different causes are supported in different ways by different sets of supporters. Catherine Walker and Adrian Sargent have presented evidence of the wide range of motivational and decision-making factors that can influence the making of a gift. Barry Knight has suggested ways in which the context of meanings in which people may give is changing and how charities will need to adapt to this.

A new culture for giving will depend on charities being clear about what they are asking for, and on donors being clear about why they are giving and what their donations will do. The re-defining of charity will require a new clarity and realism, a new contract between charities and their donors. Modern charity will be a combination of good will and good sense. One example that seems to have attracted unquestioning support is that of medical research, towards which the public has been increasingly generous over the last couple of decades. Can something be learned from this example? It would not be appropriate to delve into the history of the major role of foundations in medical research, but it might be informative to speculate about the general public's enthusiasm for the issue. Unlike the problems of poverty and deprivation, health problems are easily seen as affecting people of all classes. Moreover, giving to medical research carries a hope for the future. The costs of medical research may be high, but its value can seem beyond measure. The public accepts that government can never foot the bill sufficiently, and that a gift for medical research is an investment with tremendous returns and limitless potential benefit.

Perhaps there are clues here for the development of a future culture of giving. Many of the contributors in this book have argued that this future culture will be about charity as a commitment to sustainable change, as investment in a better future. The public's help will be vital. Charities will need to be clear about what they can do, so that donors can support them with conviction and honesty. Fundraising will be about communicating visions to donors and evolving a clear contract for what their gifts can achieve. Future charity will not be about blind faith, but about vision, clarity, honesty, and an invitation to take part in sustainable change alongside other partners such as government and business.

In response to anxieties in the voluntary sector, government is aiming to create a new culture for giving by raising awareness of community responsibility and through practical measures such as the Giving Campaign. This is not a short-term fundraising campaign but one that aims to increase knowledge, enthusiasm and behaviour in relation to giving. It represents an innovative model of partnership between government and the voluntary sector, with targets for increasing both the amounts given to charity and also the numbers of people giving. This involves action on a broad front, from promoting the role of financial advisers in providing information on charitable giving to the wealthy, to encouraging charities to reach out to all types of donor and ensure that even the smallest gifts attract the tax reliefs that the government has made available. Charities themselves also need to take a lead in offering people a vision for giving that makes sense in the modern age. Examples of charities that have begun to take steps in this direction are scattered throughout the book, but much more is needed. As Andrew Passey has highlighted, people are less likely to take charities on trust. For many people today, the virtue of charity is neither a given good nor a faith-based duty. Confidence and trust have to be built, partly through transparent and efficient use of donations, but also through faith in charitable activities.

Finally, most of the available research on the state of giving today has stemmed from the efforts and resources of voluntary organisations themselves. Government and other agencies are deriving growing benefit from this work. In Britain, the government and the voluntary sector are increasingly working together to collect and analyse such data, and it is to be hoped that this will help to put information and research about the sector on a firmer footing. In other countries, the relationship between government and the voluntary sector is closer still: StatsCan in Canada, which supports regular national data collection on giving, provides a good example of how governments can support such activity.

We hope that this book has gone a long way towards answering some of the basic and most pressing questions about giving today. It is not intended as the last word on the subject. If giving is to remain at the forefront of people's, and governments', minds, and if we are serious about encouraging greater engagement and interest, we need to develop a greater understanding of what motivates giving, of how different factors interact in decision making, and of what charitable giving means to people in a changing society. The contributors to this book have attempted to open up a new discourse and to convey a new excitement about the role of philanthropy in the twenty-first century. There are a lot of opportunities to be seized out there, and, above all, there is a lot of give.

ABOUT THE AUTHORS

Richard Fries is currently a visiting fellow at the Centre for Civil Society at the London School of Economics, where he contributes to programmes on the law and regulation of charities and other voluntary organisations. From 1992 until his retirement in 1999, he was Chief Charity Commissioner for England and Wales, and in this period he was responsible for leading the development of the Commission to fulfil its enhanced supervisory role under the Charities Act 1993. Before that, he had been a career civil servant in the Home Office, where, from 1987 to 1991, he was responsible for government policy on charity and the voluntary sector.

Les Hems is Director of Research at the Institute for Philanthropy, University College, London. The Institute for Philanthropy is currently undertaking a number of research projects relating to giving, including: analysing the behaviour of strategic philanthropists; the development of methods to evaluate and communicate impact that contributes to building donor trust and confidence; patterns of charitable giving in Great Britain 1995–2001; the evaluation of links between the regulatory environment and the development of philanthropy. The Institute has also compiled the *Giving Atlas*, a review of UK initiatives to promote philanthropy, which is available via the Institute's website and will be maintained by the Institute. Les Hems is also Consulting Associate to the Johns Hopkins International Comparative Nonprofit Sector Project with particular interest in civil society in South Asia. His recent publications include *UK Voluntary Sector Almanac 2000* (with Passey and Jas) and *Trust and Civil Society* (with Passey and Tonkiss).

Sarah Hughes has, since joining CAF in 1996, led CAF's development as a leading exponent of the internet and other new technologies in the non-profit sector. CAF currently has four core websites with a number of satellite sites serving its eight international offices, all of which provide innovative solutions and opportunities for funders and fund seekers alike. Sarah sits on a number of representative internet bodies, both in the UK and internationally, and has contributed to a wide range of articles and journals on the role of the internet in philanthropic and developmental activity. Sarah also provides consultancy and guidance to organisations in the UK and overseas. Sarah has a background in languages, marketing and business development.

Pauline Jas has been a research officer at NCVO since January 1999. She is responsible for the Individual Giving Research programme, which includes the building of the long-term dataset on charitable giving by the public, as well as the research into motivations for giving behaviour. She is also responsible for the production of the *UK Voluntary Sector Almanac 2002*, and the yearly Researching the Voluntary Sector Conference. Other research activities include labour force issues such as partnerships and social capital in the voluntary sector. Prior to working for NCVO, Pauline worked as a consumer psychologist in the food industry.

John Kingston worked as a VSO volunteer in Trinidad before reading Economics at Cambridge. Two years as an ODI Nuffield Fellow in Swaziland were followed by postgraduate study for a Master of Business Administration degree at Manchester Business School. He then joined 3i Group, an investment bank specialising in small and medium-sized businesses, before renewing his links with the voluntary sector in 1990, when he was appointed a director of Save the Children. In April, he joined CAF in a development role, particularly to explore the potential for venture funding of the voluntary sector in the UK. John is Chair of the ICFM and the Giving with Confidence project, a joint initiative of NCVO/ICFM/CAF, and has been a trustee of a number of voluntary organisations.

Barry Knight is a social scientist who has worked for Cambridge University and the Home Office. He has been the head of information and research at the London Voluntary Service Council and taught at Morley College, where he and colleagues pioneered the first 'Fresh Start' course for adults who wished to return to learning. Since 1989, Barry has worked for CENTRIS, a non-profit organisation pioneering new ways of thinking about old problems. He has written seven books about different aspects of the non-profit sector. His latest, *Reviving Democracy: citizens at the centre of governance*, written with Rajesh Tandon and Hope Chigudu, is to be published by Earthscan and the Commonwealth Foundation in 2002.

Howard Lake is a director of pioneering internet fundraising consultancy, Fundraising UK Ltd. Since 1994 he has published *UK Fundraising* (www.fundraising.co.uk), the leading internet resource for charity fundraisers and the fundraising industry. In 1996 Howard wrote the first guide to internet fundraising, *Direct Connection's Guide to Fundraising on the Internet*. A leading authority on charities' use of the internet, Howard worked for nine years as a fundraiser for Amnesty International, Afghanaid and Oxfam.

Stephen Lee is currently director of the Centre for Voluntary Sector Management and member of the marketing faculty at Henley Management College. He has been involved in the voluntary sector since 1982; he has worked at the Charities Advisory Trust, DSC, South Bank University, and ICFM, where, as director for eleven years, he established himself as a leading authority on charity fundraising, marketing, charity law, governance and ethical issues. A fellow of the RSA and one of only four Honorary Fellows of the ICFM, he received the inaugural Professional Fundraising Lifetime Achievement Award in September 2000.

Redmond Mullin is Chairman of Redmond Mullin Ltd. He has degrees in philosophy (Heythrop) and in ancient European literature (Oxford). He was formerly a Jesuit, in research at Masius, in advertising at J Walter Thompson, in fundraising with Wells, a director at CAF. He was a founder of the ICFM, a non-executive director of the London Philharmonic Orchestra, chairman of the Advisory Committee for the Open University Voluntary Sector Management Programme and of ICFM's Fellows Working Party. He is a member of WWF's Communications and Marketing Committee, and Trustee of Dartington Summer Arts Foundation.

Andrew Passey heads the Value Added team at the Office for National Statistics (ONS), which is responsible for maximising the use of new and existing ONS data across government and beyond. He was previously head of research at NCVO, where his role was to

Foundation he is responsible for the syndicated public awareness, media and parliamentary tracking services that the Future Foundation runs, as well as developing research projects on issues such as branding, outsourcing and the internet. He is co-chair of the Not-for-Profit Internet Task Force. Before Future Foundation, Joe Saxton was Director of Communications at the RNID, Britain's largest charity for deaf and hard-of-hearing people, responsible for PR, disability consultancy, lobbying, campaigning, policy, information and membership. He was with Brann, the world's largest direct marketing group for five years, and has worked with numerous charities. He co-founded the *Journal of Nonprofit* and *Voluntary Sector Marketing* and is the author of *It's Competition, but not as we know it* and *What are Charities for?*, published by Third Sector. For six years he was a trustee of the RSPCA and chair of both the Public Affairs and International committees.

Catherine Walker is Head of Research at CAF, which she joined in 1999 (having previously been at the Fairtrade Foundation and Exeter University School of Psychology). She has been heavily involved in CAF's programme of monitoring the impact of the charity tax review and subsequent changes to tax-effective charitable giving, especially the new Gift Aid scheme. Catherine carried out the first survey of UK business leaders' involvement with charities, a collaborative project with Deloitte & Touche involving senior figures in UK business. Her other current research interests include a psychological investigation of donor motivations, household decision making in giving to charity, how donors make use of the internet, and young people's engagement with charity. She has written for a variety of sector and academic journals and is co-editor of the *Handbook for the Teaching of Economic and Consumer Psychology*. Catherine is an associate editor of the *Journal of Economic Psychology* and member of the Scientific Committee for the International Association for Research in Economic Psychology.

David Wickert has been a director of Chapel & York since 1997. He is an Anglican Priest and, from 1976 to 1986, he was Vicar of Waterloo in central London. He was the first chairman of the Waterloo Trust and chairman of the Southwark Council for Social Aid. He co-founded the Upstream Theatre Club and has produced plays in West End and London Fringe, and on and off Broadway, as well as touring productions throughout the world. He has been an adviser to organisations connected with the arts and religion in the UK and the USA. Most recently he has co-authored *Fundraising from America* and edited *Directory of American Company Grantmakers* and the *Directory of Grantmakers' Websites CD Rom*.

Redmond Mullin.

I specialise in strategies for major targets,

Which usually include the biggest units of support,

And now the 'prosperous' segment.

Sums achieved are in £ millions.

To talk, without commitment, contact me at:

tel: 01647 433398 fax: 01647 433385

e-mail: REDMONDMULLIN@hotmail.com

MEMBERSHIP

USEFUL ADDRESSES

CAF

Kings Hill
West Malling
Kent
ME19 4TA
tel: 01732 520000
fax: 01732 520001
e-mail: research@CAFonline.org
websites: www.CAFonline.org
www.allaboutgiving.org

The Charity Commission

website: www.charity-commission.gov.uk

London
Hamsworth House
13–15 Bouverie Street
London
EC4Y 8DP
tel: 0870 333 0123
fax: 020 7674 2300
Central register open 0900–1700

Taunton
Woodfield House
Tangier
Taunton
Somerset
TA1 4BL
tel: 0870 333 0123
fax: 01823 345003
Central register open 0900–1600

Liverpool
20 Kings Parade
Queen's Dock
Liverpool
L3 4DQ

tel: as above
fax: 0151 703 1555
Central register open 0900–1630

Hearing- and speech-impaired callers using minicom: 0870 333 0125

Charity Finance Directors Group

Camelford House
87–89 Albert Embankment
London
SE1 7TP
tel: 020 7793 1400
fax: 020 7793 1600
e-mail: mail@cfdg.org.uk
website: www.cfdg.org.uk

Future Foundation

70 Cowcross Street
London
EC1M 6DG
tel: 020 7250 3343
fax: 020 7251 8138
e-mail: info@futurefoundation.net
websites: www.futurefoundation.net
www.futurefoundation.net/notforprofit/toppage.htm

The Giving Campaign

6th Floor
Haymarket House
1a Oxenden Street
London
SW1Y 4EE
tel: 020 7930 3154
fax: 020 7925 0985
e-mail: admin@givingcampaign.org.uk
website: www.givingcampaign.org.uk

Inland Revenue

website: www.open.gov.uk/inrev

Helplines:
Gift Aid: 0151 472 6038/6055/6056

Payroll giving: 0151 472 6029/6053
Gifts of stocks and securities: 0151 472 6043/6046
fax: 0151 472 6268/6060

Inland Revenue (Charities) Repayments
St Johns House
Merton Road
Bootle
Merseyside
L69 9BB

For Scotland
Inland Revenue (Charities)
Meldrum House
15 Drumsheugh Gardens
Edinburgh
EH3 7UL
tel: 0131 777 4040
fax: 0131 777 4045

Institute for Fiscal Studies

3rd Floor
7 Ridgmount Street
London
WC1E 7AE
tel: 020 7291 4800
fax: 020 7323 4780
e-mail: mailbox@ifs.organisation.uk
website: www.ifs.org.uk

Institute of Charity Fundraising Managers (ICFM)
Market Towers
1 Nine Elms Lane
London
SW8 5NQ
tel: 020 7627 3436
fax: 020 7627 3508
e-mail: enquiries@icfm.co.uk
website: www.icfm.org.uk

NCVO

Regents Wharf
8 All Saints Street
London
N1 9RL
tel: 020 7713 6161
fax: 020 7713 6300
minicom: 0800 0188111
helpdesk: 0800 2798 798
e-mail: ncvo@ncvo-vol.org.uk
website: www.ncvo-vol.org.uk

UK Fundraising

Fundraising UK Ltd
36 Palestine Grove
London
SW19 2QN
tel: 020 8640 5233
e-mail: hlake@fundraising.co.uk
website: www.fundraising.co.uk

ABOUT CAF

CAF, Charities Aid Foundation, is a registered charity with a unique mission – to increase the substance of charity in the UK and overseas. It provides services that are both charitable and financial which help donors make the most of their giving and charities make the most of their resources.

As an integral part of its activities, CAF works to raise standards of management in voluntary organisations. This includes the making of grants by its own Grants Council, sponsorship of the Charity Annual Report and Accounts Awards, seminars, training courses and the Charities Annual Conference, the largest regular gathering of key people from within the voluntary sector. In addition, Charitynet (www.charitynet.org) is now established as the leading internet site on voluntary action.

For decades, CAF has led the way in developing tax-effective services to donors, and these are now used by more than 250,000 individuals and 2,000 of the UK's leading companies, between them giving £150 million each year to charity. Many are also using CAF's CharityCard, the world's first debit card designed exclusively for charitable giving. CAF's unique range of investment and administration services for charities includes the CafCash High Interest Cheque Account, two common investment funds for longer-term investment and a full appeals and subscription management service.

CAF's activities are not limited to the UK, however. Increasingly, CAF is looking to apply the same principles and develop similar services internationally, in its drive to increase the substance of charity across the world. CAF has offices and sister organisations in the United States, Bulgaria, South Africa, Russia, India and Brussels.

CAF Research is a leading source of information and research on the voluntary sector's income and resources. Its annual publication, *Dimensions of the Voluntary Sector,* provides year-on-year updates and its Research Report series covers a wide range of topics, including costs benchmarking, partnership resources, and trust and company funding. More details on research and publications may be found on www.CAFonline.org/research

For more information about CAF, please visit www.CAFonline.org/

ABOUT NCVO

The National Council for Voluntary Organisations (NCVO) is the umbrella body for the voluntary sector in England, with sister councils in Wales, Scotland and Northern Ireland.

NCVO has a growing membership of over 2,000 voluntary organisations, ranging from large national bodies to community groups, volunteer bureaux and development agencies working at local level.

NCVO is a highly effective lobbying organisation and represents the views of its members and the wider voluntary sector to government, the Charity Commission, the EU and other bodies. It is also at the leading edge of research into, and analysis of, the voluntary sector – its work in this area carries considerable weight with policy makers.

NCVO publishes the *UK Voluntary Sector Almanac* bi-annually, a comprehensive analysis of the economic contribution of the voluntary sector, which provides voluntary organisations with the vital understanding of the changing environment in which they operate and the key trends within the sector.

NCVO also provides high quality information and advice to voluntary organisations, through its Helpdesk, publications, *voluntary*sector magazine, events, and information networks. To help voluntary organisations make the best use of limited funds, NCVO also offers a range of money-saving deals on key services of use to charities or voluntary groups.

NCVO has been instrumental in the initiative that resulted in the Giving Campaign, and retains an active interest and involvement at all levels of the campaign.

NCVO's annual conference has rapidly established itself as the premier event in the voluntary sector calendar.

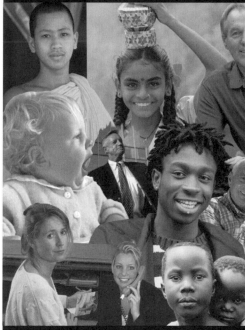